500 Handmade Books

500 HANDMADE BOOKS

INSPIRING INTERPRETATIONS OF A TIMELESS FORM

LARK
BOOKS

A Division of
Sterling Publishing Co., Inc.
New York / London

SENIOR EDITOR: **Suzanne J. E. Tourtillott**

EDITORS: **Julie Hale, Chris Rich**

ART DIRECTOR: **Jackie Kerr**

COVER DESIGNER: **Cindy LaBreacht**

FRONT COVER
Laura Wait
Abstract Illegible #1, 2005
Photo by artist

BACK COVER, FROM TOP LEFT
Laura Wait
X, Letter of Danger, Sex and the Unknown, Vol. 1, 2006
Photo by artist

Debra Fink Bachelder
Head Case, 2004
Photo by artist

Harriete Estel Berman
And There Was Light, 2004
Photo by Philip Cohen

Peter Thomas
Donna Thomas
Y2K3MS: Ukulele Series Book #2, Ukulele Accordion, 1996
Photo by Rob Thomas

SPINE
Laura Russell
Simplify, 2004
Photo by artist

FRONT FLAP, FROM TOP
Sharon McCartney
A Constant Sound of Birds, 2004
Photo by John Polak Photography

Susan Collard
The Winter Palace, 2006
Photo by artist

BACK FLAP, FROM TOP
Karen Koshgarian
September 11—A Memorial, 2005
Photo by Artist

Erin Zamrzla
Untitled, 2006
Photo by artist

Liz Mitchell
9 x 9, 2004
Photo by Craig Phillips

PAGE 3
Alice Austin
Red, Yellow, Blue, 2000
Photo by artist

PAGE 5
Alice M. Vinson
Keep Out, 2003
Photo by artist

Library of Congress Cataloging-in-Publication Data

500 handmade books : inspiring interpretations of a timeless form/
[developing editor, Suzanne J. E. Tourtillott; editor, Linda Kopp].
     p. cm.
   Includes index.
   ISBN-13: 978-1-57990-877-5 (pbk. : alk. paper)
   ISBN-10: 1-57990-877-2 (pbk. : alk. paper)
   1. Book design. I. Tourtillott, Suzanne J. E. II. Kopp, Linda. III.
Title: Five hundred handmade books.
   Z246.A14 2008
   686—dc22

                                    2007046347

10 9 8 7 6 5 4

Published by Lark Books, A Division of
Sterling Publishing Co., Inc.
387 Park Avenue South, New York, NY 10016

Text © 2008, Lark Books, A Division of Sterling Publishing Co., Inc.;
unless otherwise specified
Photography © 2008, Artist/Photographer

Distributed in Canada by Sterling Publishing,
c/o Canadian Manda Group, 165 Dufferin Street
Toronto, Ontario, Canada M6K 3H6

Distributed in the United Kingdom by GMC Distribution Services,
Castle Place, 166 High Street, Lewes, East Sussex, England BN7 1XU

Distributed in Australia by Capricorn Link (Australia) Pty Ltd.,
P.O. Box 704, Windsor, NSW 2756 Australia

If you have questions or comments about this book, please contact:

Lark Books, 67 Broadway, Asheville, NC 28801, 828-253-0467

Manufactured in China

ISBN-13: 978-1-57990-877-5

For information about custom editions, special sales, premium and corporate
purchases, please contact Sterling Special Sales Department at 800-805-5489
or specialsales@sterlingpub.com.

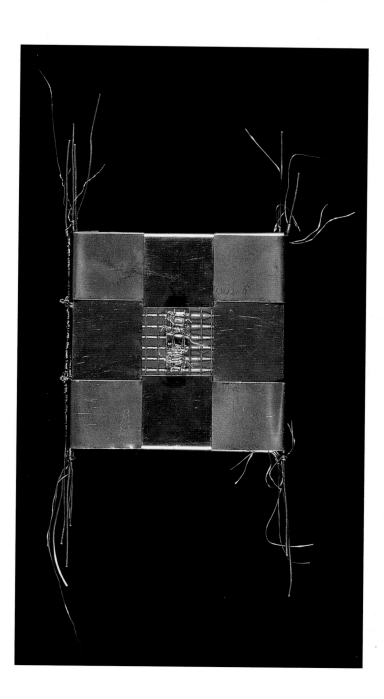

Contents

Introduction

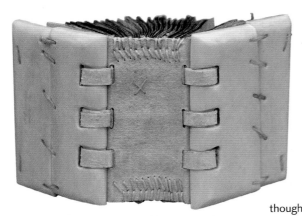

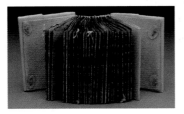

Shanna Leino
Dear Ben Brown Eyes | 2005

Dear reader, you are in for a treat. Contained within these covers is a delightful and diverse sampling of handmade books—a collection that demonstrates the incredible scope of the craft.

When I sat down to select the handmade books featured in this volume, I was astonished by the variety of submissions, and by the ingenuity and creativity of the people who produced them. Working with the editorial staff of Lark Books for the better part of a week and surveying thousands of images was a challenging yet exhilarating experience. Because there were so many remarkable books to choose from, we quickly realized that boundaries for the collection had to be established. Of course we wanted pieces that were well made, carefully thought out, and finely crafted, with parts that worked together harmoniously. Of course we wanted each piece to reflect the heart and mind of its maker through its materials, media, and production values. But ultimately, in order to qualify, a piece had to demonstrate what we called "bookness," meaning that it had to operate like a book, opening up and presenting a sequence or potential sequence of images, words, or ideas. By this definition, a sculpture that looked like a book would not make the grade. Nor would a diptych that opened up and presented a painting or drawing.

The pieces shown in this volume represent "bookness" at its best. Capturing the range and depth of contemporary bookmaking, this collection is a testament to the flexibility of the craft. The work included here varies from simple and austere to dazzlingly complex, from sweet and childlike to dark and moody. There are beautifully crafted blank books and pieces that feature elaborate, content-driven narratives. Some books are traditional; others are outrageous. Many of the books feature cover and binding structures that serve as sculptures or paintings instead of simply protecting the pages they contain.

If I had to select one handmade book that embodies the inspiration behind this collection, it would be Shanna Leino's *Dear Ben Brown Eyes*, a fantasy work composed of elk bone, handmade paper, and linen thread. At first sight, the piece took my breath away. This simple book—a treasure that fits into the palm of a hand—combines historically traditional materials with Leino's confident artistry. The piece possesses an energy that radiates from centuries of devotion to the book form. It's the work of a bookmaker who loves the craft and is deeply experienced in the practice of it.

Another standout piece, Alice Simpson's *Urban Motion*, is a thrilling hip-hop-sequenced accordion structure that comes blasting out of a raw, painted cover. The brilliant hues, rough encaustic cover work, and ramped-up drawings lure the viewer in. Equally stunning is Harry Reese's *Funagainstawake*, a piece that's shocking in its utter simplicity and rightness, inside and out. The white space around the type and the image, the perfection of the type inscribed on the handmade paper, and the fit of the binding make this book a sort of minimalist landscape.

When it comes to the whimsical and playful, Judith A. Hoffman's *7 Extinction Events* brings down the house. A book that pops out of a dinosaur is simply too exciting not to be included in this collection. Another fun piece is Mary Howe's *ABZ Bees*, an ingeniously designed package that features superb examples of different bookmaking techniques, including collage, flip, and pop-up.

Participating in this project gave me the rare opportunity to see what book artists are doing today. I am grateful to all of the individuals who submitted their work for consideration. It's heartening to know that, in this digital age, handmade books are being recognized as vessels of humanized content, touchstones of what we are as people. It's clear that bookmakers are having one heck of a good time doing what they do best—slowing down and making wonderful pieces by hand. I believe that if you touched these books, you could feel their creators—devoted artists who are carrying on a wonderful and enduring tradition.

Steve Miller, Juror

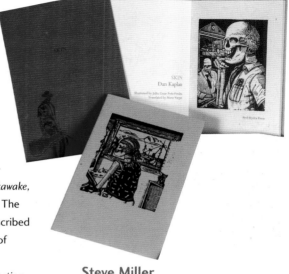

Steve Miller
Skin by Dan Kaplan, translated by Maria Vargas | 2005

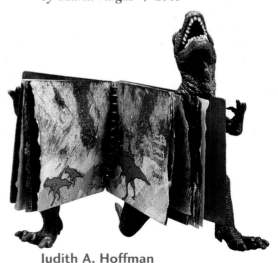

Judith A. Hoffman
7 Extinction Events | 2006

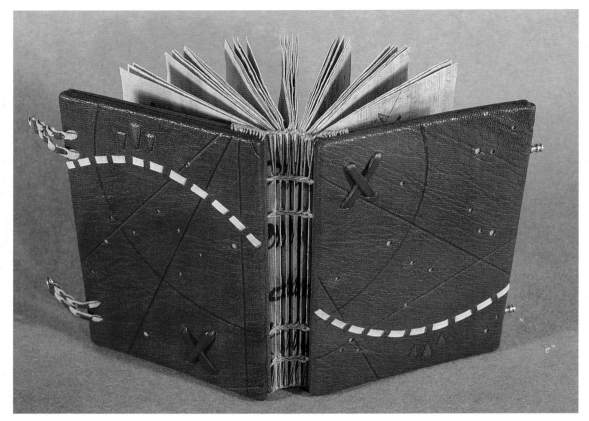

Bonnie Stahlecker

Windows in Time | 2004

5½ X 3¾ INCHES (14 X 9.5 CM)

Calf leather, vellum, papyrus; Ethiopian Coptic stitch,
Coptic headbands; inkjet printed

PHOTOS BY ARTIST

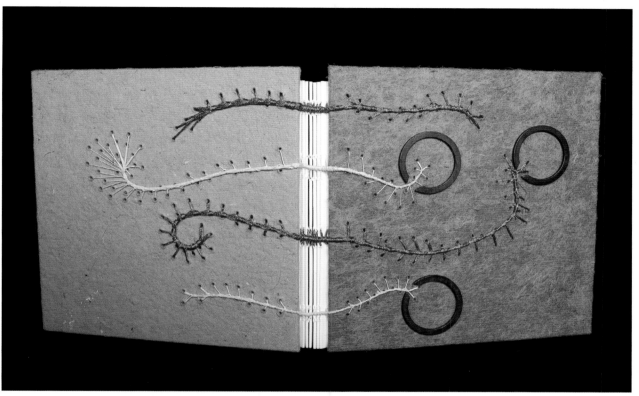

E. Bond

Fault Lines | 2006

7 1/8 X 7 1/8 X 3/4 INCHES (14.6 X 6.4 X 2.8 CM)

Handmade paper; caterpillar binding; recycled metal pieces, linen and metallic thread

PHOTOS BY SIOBHAN EDMONDS

Jody Alexander

The Flight of Mrs. Viola D. Pigeon | 2003

6 X 4½ X 1½ INCHES (15.2 X 11.4 X 3.8 CM)
Kozo and gampi blend paper; encaustic;
packed sewing over split thongs binding

PHOTO BY ARTIST

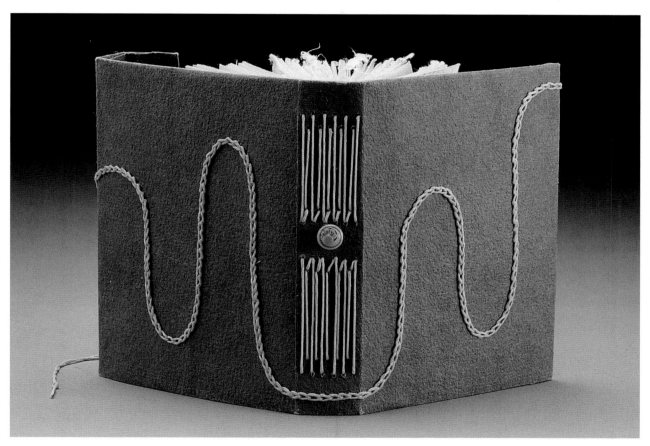

Michelle Francis
Untitled | 2004

5 X 3³/₄ X 1 INCHES (12.7 X 9.5 X 2.5 CM)
Flax, Thai paper, paste paper, waxed linen
thread, vintage button; long stitch binding
PHOTO BY TOM MILLS

Susan Carol Messer
Side by Side | 2006

7 X 5¼ X 1 INCHES (17.8 X 13.3 X 2.5 CM)
Handmade paper from kapok fiber, artist's hair, brass,
textbook image; codex binding; carved, hand cut

PHOTOS BY ARTIST

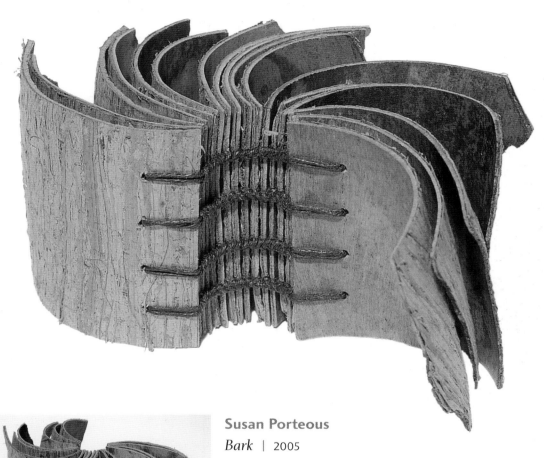

Susan Porteous

Bark | 2005

2½ X 2½ X 1½ INCHES (6.4 X 6.4 X 3.8 CM)
Bark, papyrus, waxed linen thread; single-sheet
Coptic binding; photocopied

PHOTOS BY ARTIST

Daniel Essig

Book in a Book | 2005

5 X 3½ X 3 INCHES (12.7 X 8.9 X 7.6 CM)

Mahogany, handmade paper, milk paint, mica, fossils, tin; Greek binding

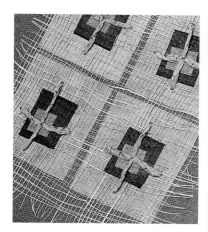

Nancy Pobanz
GridLock | 2005

7³/₄ X 6¹/₂ X 1³/₄ INCHES
(19.7 X 16.5 X 4.4 CM)

Handmade paper, abaca cloth, canvas,
acrylic inks, earth pigments, graphite,
painted and waxed linen threads;
accordion binding; painted, collage,
handwritten, pen and ink

PHOTOS BY LIGHTWORKS PHOTOGRAPHY

Pati Scobey

Xok | 2003

CLOSED: 6 X 2 X ½ INCHES (6 X 5 X 1.3 CM)
Acrylic and wax on binders board;
slip book structure

PHOTOS BY ARTIST

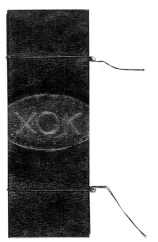

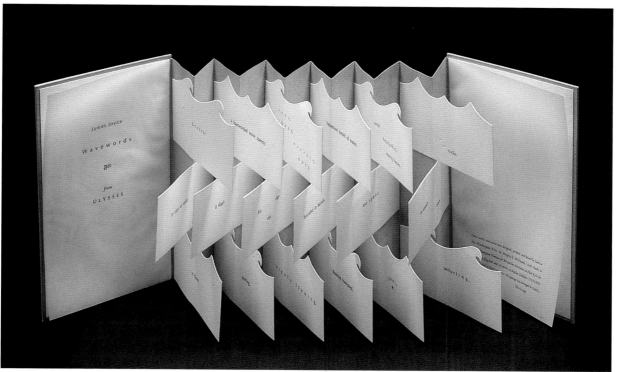

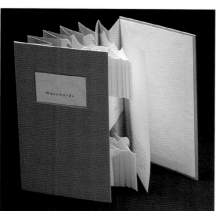

Margery S. Hellmann

Wavewords | 1996

CLOSED: 7³/₄ X 4⁵/₈ X ¹/₂ INCHES (19.7 X 11.8 X 1.3 CM)

Rives BFK, UV ultra, Strathmore 500 papers; paper over boards binding; flag book, die cut; letterpress, handset type, suminagashi

PHOTOS BY ARTIST

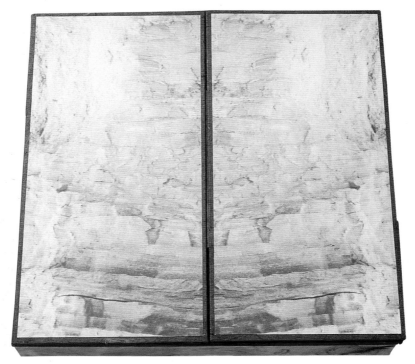

Shellie Jacobson

Breathe | 2005

6 X 6 X 1 INCHES (15.2 X 15.2 X 2.5 CM)

Mohawk, Moriki, Strathmore; clay;
Jacob's Ladder hinge

PHOTOS BY CRAIG PHILLIPS

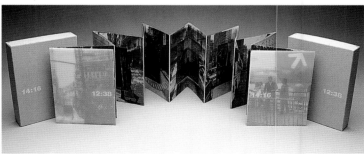

Cynthia Lollis
Daniela Deeg
12:38-14:16 | 2006

7⁷/₈ X 5⁷/₈ X 1³/₈ INCHES (20 X 15 X 3.5 CM)

Gmund paper, acetate, clear plastic sheeting, linen thread, grayboard box; star accordion binding; screen printed

PHOTOS BY WALKER MONTGOMERY

Liz Mitchell

9 x 9 | 2004

1¼ X 19¾ INCHES (3.2 X 50.2 CM)

Arches paper, clear plastic sheeting;
accordion binding; monoprint

PHOTO BY CRAIG PHILLIPS

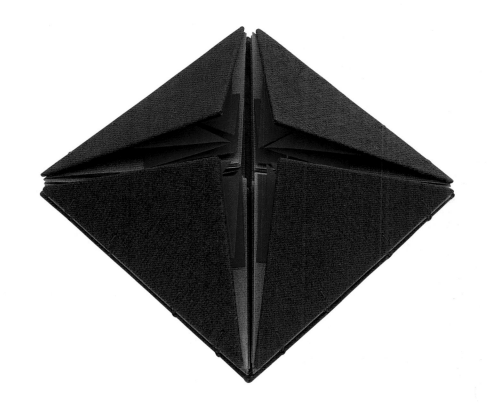

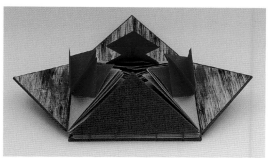

Ingrid Hein Borch

Lotus Squared | 2006

6 11/16 X 6 11/16 X 3/4 INCHES (16.9 X 16.9 X 1.9 CM)

Handmade paper, book board, linen thread, acid-free paper, paste paper; Coptic binding

PHOTOS BY ALBERT J. BORCH

Alice Austin

Red, Yellow, Blue | 2000

10 X 5 X 3 INCHES (25.4 X 12.7 X 7.6 CM)

Paste paper; map fold; offset lithography

PHOTO BY ARTIST

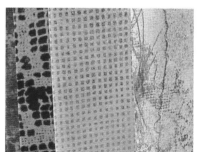

Allison Cooke Brown

Core Sample | 2003

CLOSED: 5 X 4¼ X 1 INCHES (12.7 X 10.9 X 2.5 CM)
Paper, double star book with slipcase, paste paper;
photocopy lithography, letterpress label

PHOTOS BY DEAN POWELL

Erin B. Gray

Cereology II | 2004

5¼ X 7¼ X 1 INCHES (13.3 X 18.4 X 2.5 CM)

Copper, lead-free enamel, handmade paper, waxed linen, ink, wood, Limoges enamel; Coptic binding; drawn, painted, smoked edges

PHOTOS BY TIM BARNWELL

Steven Hendricks
Breathing Mac | 2000

7 X 9 X ¾ INCHES (17.8 X 22.9 X 1.9 CM)
Lotka paper; long stitch; letterpress

Elizabeth Rotchford-Long

Winnow | 2005

5 X 5½ INCHES (12.7 X 14 CM)

Handmade paper, husk fiber, vellum, printmaking paper; accordion binding; monoprint, hand marbled, embossed, solvent transfer

PHOTOS BY D. J. EVANS

Janice Spillane
Meditation | 2005

6½ X 9½ X ⅜ INCHES (16.5 X 24.1 X 0.9 CM)

Paper, magazine ads, foil paper, Shoji, silk thread, metal button, polymer clay; stab binding; stamped, pressed, embossed

PHOTO BY RICHARD WOZNIAK

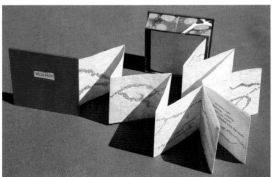

Katrin Kapp Braun

Woman | 2006

2¹⁵/₁₆ X 2¹⁵/₁₆ X 1³/₁₆ INCHES (7.5 X 7.5 X 3 CM)

Cotton-abaca paper, Hahnemühle Biblio paper, mulberry paper, Turkish paper, binders board; accordian binding; letterpress

PHOTOS BY ARTIST

Lisa Rappoport

A Flame in the Heart | 2002

CLOSED: 11 X 7 INCHES (27.9 X 17.8 CM)

Johannot, Thai Unryu papers, reversible covers, paste-paper liners; accordion binding; letterpress, handset type

PHOTO BY ARTIST

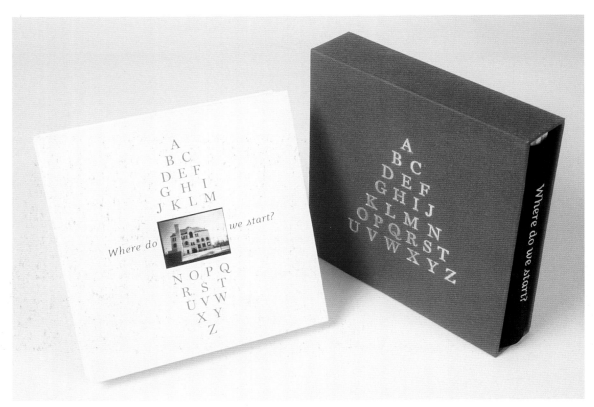

Wilber H. Schilling

Where Do We Start? | 2003

6 X 6 X 1½ INCHES (15.2 X 15.2 X 3.8 CM)

Hahnemühle paper, cloth, paper; accordion and dos-a-dos binding; letterpess, inkjet printed, foil stamped

PHOTOS BY ARTIST

Bettina Pauly

Fragile | 2006

37 X 16½ INCHES (94 X 41.9 CM)

Bookcloth, Lokta paper, cotton ribbon; assembled

PHOTO BY ARTIST

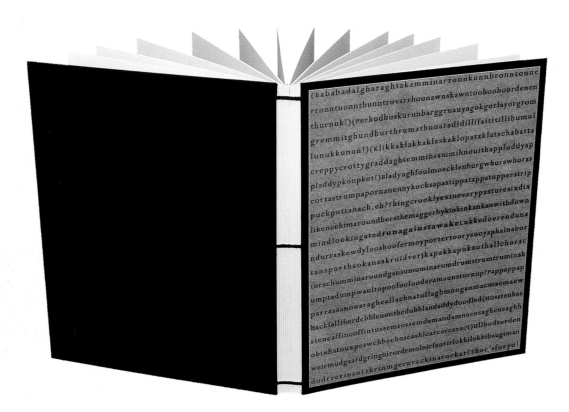

Harry Reese

Funagainstawake | 1997

12¼ X 9¼ X 1 INCHES (31.1 X 23.5 X 2.5 CM)

Magnani's Italia paper; wire-edge binding; monotype prints from hand-painted vinyl, letterpress, handset type, photoengraving, polymer plates

PHOTOS BY DOUG FARRELL

Michelle Francis

B Is for Book | 2006

5 X 5³/₄ X 2³/₄ INCHES (12.7 X 14.6 X 7 CM)

Lokta, flax, folio, hand- and machine-marbled papers, waxed and unwaxed linen thread, mixed media; concertina binding; stamped, laser printed

Shu-Ju Wang

Fatherland | 2006

CLOSED: 4½ X 6¾ X ¼ INCHES (11.4 X 17.2 X 0.6 CM)

Rives lightweight, Taiwanese handmade paper;
accordion binding; Gocco printed

PHOTOS BY ARTIST

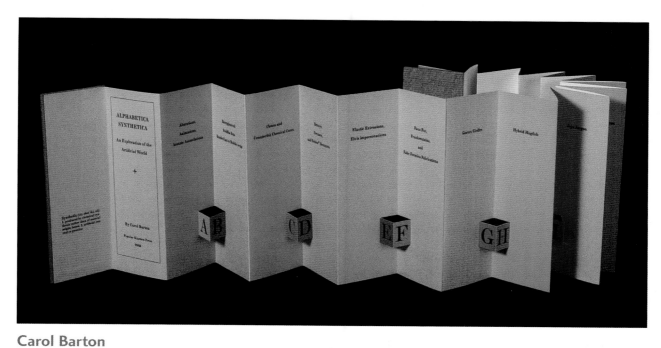

Carol Barton

Alphabetica Synthetica | 2003

7 X 2½ X 70 INCHES (17.8 X 6.4 X 177.8 CM)

Book board; accordion fold; pop-ups, laser printed

PHOTO BY ARTIST

Alice Simpson

Evils of the Dance | 2003

8½ X 29 X ½ INCHES (21.6 X 73.7 X 1.3 CM)

Astrobright paper, embroidery thread;
accordion binding; photocopied

PHOTO BY D. JAMES DEE

Patricia T. Hetzler

Woman of Substance | 2004

7½ X 6½ X 1 INCHES (19 X 16.5 X 2.5 CM)

Fabriano Uno, Canson, Thai Unryu, decorative, text-weight, and waxed papers; accordion binding; hand sewn, rubber stamped, pasted

PHOTOS BY MORRIS C. HETZLER

Lorraine Lamothe

Secular Prayer Book No. 5: Psychological Baggage | 2005

3 1/8 X 9 X 7/16 INCHES (8 X 23 X 1 CM)

Found paper and ephemera; pasted, stamped, dry letter transfer, drawn

PHOTO BY LIGHTWAVE PHOTOGRAPHY

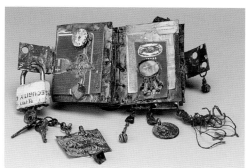

Juliana Coles

Uncharted Depths | 2000

3 X 4¼ X 2 INCHES (7.6 X 10.8 X 5 CM)

Copper sheeting, found metal hardware, jewelry, washers, paper collage, tin scraps, copper wire, lock and keys; dipped in silver tarnishing solution

PHOTOS BY PAT BERRETT

Linda O'Brien
Opie O'Brien

Dios De La Muerte | 2005

CLOSED: 3¹/₄ X 3¹/₄ X 1¹/₂ INCHES (8.3 X 8.3 X 3.8 CM)

Gourd covers, steel, copper, tin, silver, amate and gourd pulp papers, leather, wax, coins, beads, stamps, bezel, cabochon; accordion binding; wood burned, rubber stamped, metal formed, embossed

PHOTOS BY DINA ROSSI

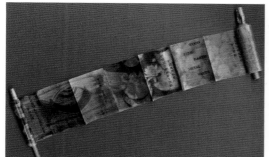

Jackie Richards
7 Pillars of Tao | 2006

CLOSED: 2¹/₂ X 1³/₄ X ¹/₄ INCHES (6.4 X 4.4 X 0.6 CM);
OPEN: 28 INCHES (71.1 CM)

Paper, fiber, encaustics base,
seashell; etched, altered rusted hinge,
hand-forged chain

PHOTOS BY ARTIST

Dorothy A. Yule

A Book for Ian | 2006

3¹/₂ X 2¹/₂ X 1³/₄ INCHES (8.9 X 6.4 X 4.4 CM)

Mohawk Superfine, Joss papers, rose petals, gold thread, magnetic closure; concertina binding; letterpress, laser printed, hand colored, sewn

PHOTOS BY ARTIST

Marilyn R. Rosenberg

Muse | 2004

CLOSED: 12 X 15½ INCHES (30.5 X 39.4 CM)

Hard covers, gouache, thread, found objects, ink;
handmade two-ring metal binding

PHOTO BY ARTIST

Theresa Harsma

Untitled | 2003

3 3/8 X 4 X 1 3/8 INCHES (8.6 X 10.2 X 3.5 CM)
Waxed linen, Davey board, handmade paste paper;
Coptic binding, Ethiopian binding
PHOTO BY ARTIST

Maria Winkler
Le Cirque | 2002

CLOSED: 3 ½ X 3 ½ X ¾ INCHES (8.9 X 8.9 X 1.9 CM);
OPEN: 5 ½ X 26 X 4 ½ INCHES (14 X 66 X 11.4 CM)

Colored paper, cardstock; origami folded; printed

PHOTOS BY ARTIST

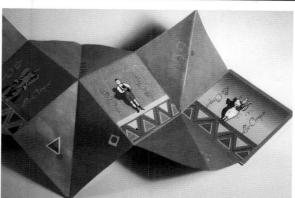

Carolyn I. Skei

Crushed Helix: Coptic and Clay Book Series | 2005

2³/₄ X 2⁷/₈ X 1 INCHES (7 X 7.3 X 2.5 CM)

Polymer clay covers, linen thread; Coptic binding, eight signatures, single-needle Coptic stitch; stamped, crushed helix pattern

PHOTOS BY ARTIST

David John Lawrence

The Four Gospels | 2006

10¹/₈ X 8¹/₈ X 1³/₄ INCHES (25.6 X 20.9 X 4.3 CM)

Goatskin, leather, calfskin, kangaroo skin,
23-karat gold leaf; stamped, molded, embroidered

PHOTO BY BOBBY BADGER

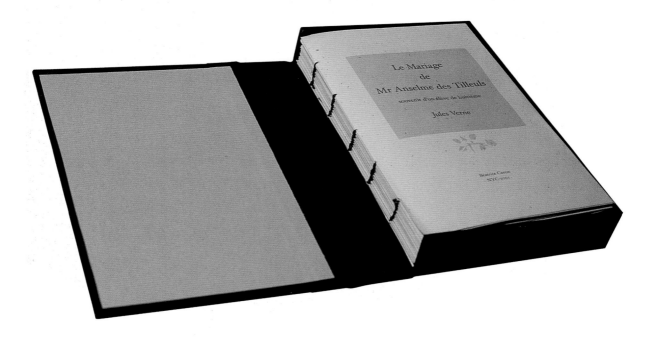

Béatrice Coron

Le Mariage d'Anselme des Tilleuls | 2001

9 X 6 X 1 INCHES (22.9 X 15.2 X 2.5 CM)

Quest paper, bookcloth, linen thread; Coptic binding;
stenciled, inkjet printed

PHOTO BY ARTIST

Marie C. Oedel

5 Millimeters and Box | 2002

6³/₁₆ X 4⁵/₈ X ⁷/₈ INCHES (15.8 X 11.8 X 2.2 CM) EACH

Paste paper, Mohawk vellum, linen thread,
leather; hand bound, hand sewn

PHOTO BY DEAN POWELL

The Jewelry Box

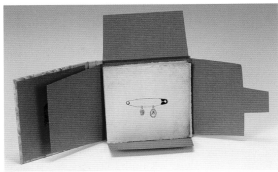

Laurie Corral

The Jewelry Box | 2000

4½ X 5 X ½ INCHES
(11.4 X 12.7 X 1.3 CM)

Paste paper, Canson,
Rives BFK, cloth; portfolio,
loose pages; Gocco printed,
rubber stamped, etched

PHOTOS BY ARTIST

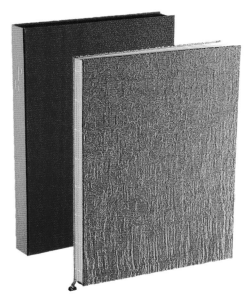

Harriet Bart

Punica Granatum | 2005

14 X 10½ X 1³⁄₁₆ INCHES (35.6 X 26.7 X 3 CM)

Masonite boards, silken fabric, silk hinges;
Coptic binding; letterpress, embossed

PHOTOS BY RIK SFERRA

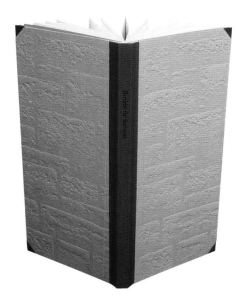

Wilber H. Schilling

*Bartleby the Scrivener:
A Story of Wall Street* | 1995

12 X 6 X ¾ INCHES (30.5 X 15.2 X 1.9 CM)

Arches MBM paper; sewn boards binding;
debossed and etched covers, magnesium plate,
foil stamping; letterpress, handset type,
polymer plates; lettering by Suzanne Moore

PHOTOS BY ARTIST

Mindy Belloff

Ten Reflections on Rainer Maria Rilke's Duino Elegies | 2002

10^1/$_2$ X 7^1/$_2$ X ^{3}/$_8$ INCHES (26.7 X 19 X 1 CM)

Original gouache, pigment and ink paintings, archival rag paper;
binding by Judith Ivry; digital printing, hand painted, collage

PHOTOS BY ARTIST

Macy Chadwick
Lisa Onstad

Aggregate Memory | 2005

8 5/8 X 5 1/4 X 1/4 INCHES (21.9 X 13.3 X 0.6 CM)

Gasen and Hanji papers, hard covers;
leporello two-sided accordion binding;
letterpress, pressure prints, relief prints, polymer plates;
text by Lisa Onstad and Macy Chadwick; cloth-covered box

PHOTOS BY MACY CHADWICK

A bitter longing grows
an ache
spreading over the present moment

Sam Garriott Antonacci

Seattle Skyline | 2004

4½ X 3¼ X 1 INCHES (11.4 X 8.3 X 2.5 CM)

Arches, Prismacolor papers; accordion binding

PHOTOS BY ROGER SCHREIBER
PRIVATE COLLECTION

Emily Gold

These Walls | 2005

CLOSED: 6¼ X 5½ INCHES (15.9 X 14 CM)

Canson and Mohawk superfine papers, handmade
paper; carousel book; collage, hand stitched

PHOTOS BY STEVEN TRUBITT

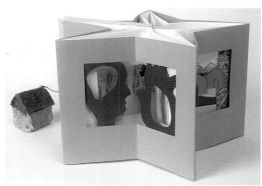

Shellie Jacobson

Message Inside | 2002

6 X 4³/₄ X 4¹/₂ INCHES (15.2 X 12 X 11.4 CM)

Rives paper, Moriki, Mylar, Iris bookcloth, tape; machine stitched, drawn

PHOTOS BY CRAIG PHILLIPS

domestic bliss

Jana C. Perez
Domestic Bliss | 2004

UNFOLDED: 55 X 9½ X 3 INCHES (139.7 X 24.1 X 7.6 CM);
FOLDED: 8 X 9½ X 5 INCHES (20.3 X 24.1 X 12.7 CM)

Photocopied magazine ads; accordion binding;
computer-generated typography

PHOTOS BY ARTIST

Geraldine A. Newfry

Homage to Audubon | 2005

9 X 6 X 2 INCHES (22.9 X 15.2 X 5 CM)

Polymer clay, found objects, copper, branches, feathers, child's block;
Coptic binding; hand etched, liquid polymer sgraffito

PHOTOS BY LARRY SANDERS

Gena M. Ollendieck

The Open Door | 2004

12 X 14 X 5 INCHES (30.5 X 35.6 X 12.7 CM)

Stonehenge and handmade paper, calf leather, cotton cord, found objects; long stitch multi-signature binding; inlaid, screw and elastic closure

PHOTO BY LARRY SANDERS

Peter Madden

Memento Mori and Misguided Angels | 1992

LEFT: 13 X 9 X 2 INCHES (33 X 22.9 X 5 CM)
RIGHT: 15 X 9 X 2 INCHES (38.1 X 22.9 X 5 CM)

Slate, copper, brass, wood, cotton, paper;
modified Japanese side-sewn binding

PHOTO BY DANA SALVO

Peter Madden

Various Binding Experiments | 1995–2000

7 X 5–18 X 12 INCHES (17.8 X 12.7–45.7 X 30.5 CM)

Slate, copper, wood, cotton, handmade paper;
accordion and Japanese side-sewn variations

PHOTO BY CLEMENTS/HOWCROFT

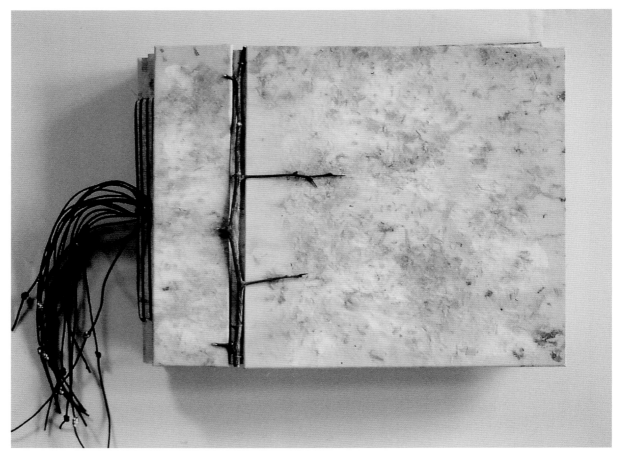

Sandy Webster

Artist Retreat Book | 2005

8 X 10 X 2 INCHES (20.3 X 25.4 X 5 CM)

Altered papers, cloth, paint, graphite, found objects; double paged, long stitch; painted, written, stitched, tied

PHOTOS BY ARTIST

Rolando Shaw

Brick Book #1, Rear | 2006

3 5/8 X 4 3/8 X 1 1/4 INCHES (9.2 X 11.1 X 3.2 CM)

Smoke-fired refractory brick, tar paper, hemp twine

PHOTO BY ARTIST

Julie L. Johnson

Aleta | 2005

6½ X 5 X 1 INCHES (16.5 X 12.7 X 2.5 CM)
Handmade sisal, gampi, kozo and papyrus paper,
artist's black and white photographs, linen,
cedar bark, dock, crocosmia; dos-a-dos binding;
Keith Smith side-bow spine stitching
PHOTOS BY BRUCE MCCAMMON

Katherine Rhodes Fields

Is blood thicker than water? | 2003

5¼ X 4¾ X 1¼ INCHES (13.3 X 12.1 X 3.2 CM)

Resin-coated photo paper, vellum, crochet thread, PVA glue, acrylic paint, and skins; buttonhole stitching; silver gelatin; ink drawings and text

PHOTOS BY ARTIST

Jody Alexander

Lost Whispers IV | 2001

6 X 4¹/₂ X ¹/₂ INCHES (15.2 X 11.4 X 1.3 CM)

Gampi and Kozo paper; hemp thread and cord

PHOTO BY ARTIST

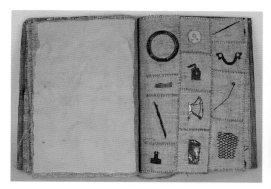

Peter Madden

Scrap Book | 1995

24 X 19 X 4 INCHES (61 X 48.3 X 10.2 CM)

Scrap wood, twine, beeswax, burlap,
scrap metal; sewn

PHOTOS BY DANA SALVO

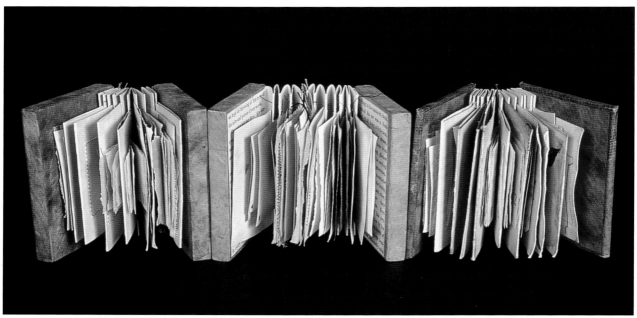

Susan Weinz

Leafage Series | 2005

4 X 3 X 2 INCHES (10.2 X 7.6 X 5 CM) EACH

Stonehenge, handmade, Super, and tracing papers, reclaimed book, wood, leaves; concertina binding, hand and machine stitching; mixed media, stamped, solvent transfers

PHOTOS BY PEGGY MCKENNA

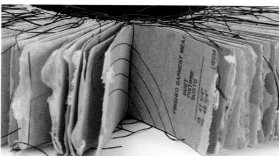

Erica Spitzer Rasmussen
Collar #2: Book of Measures | 2005

2 X 10 X 10 INCHES (5 X 25.4 X 25.4 CM)

Cotton, flax, dress pattern paper, matte medium,
waxed linen thread, Velcro; pamphlet stitched

PHOTOS BY PETRONELLA YTSMA

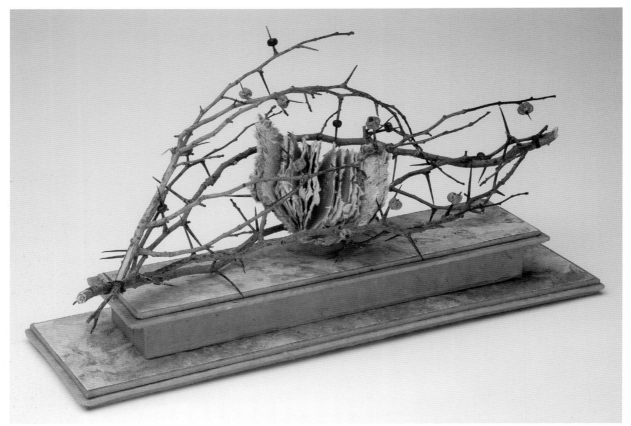

Susan Kapuscinski Gaylord

Spirit Book #13: Hope Offering | 1998

7 X 13³/₄ X 8¹/₂ INCHES (17.8 X 34.9 X 21.6 CM)

Mexican amatyl paper, Lokta paper, glass seed beads, thread, twigs, seed pods, horn beads, binders board; multiple-signature book sewn on tapes

PHOTOS BY DEAN POWELL

Bonnie O'Connell

Spinal Torsion | 2002

18 X 3 X 6 INCHES (45.7 X 7.6 X 15.2 CM)

Handmade paper, Abaca, recycled art papers,
prairie grass, linen tapes, pine needles, steel
pen nibs; hand sewn, studded

PHOTOS BY LARRY GAWELL

Laura Ann Morris

Epiphany | *2004*

9 X 7½ X 3 INCHES (22.9 X 19 X 7.6 CM)

Handmade clay slab spine,
handmade paper, yarn, feathers,
found objects; stained, stamped

PHOTO BY KRISTI FOSTER

Jeanne Germani

Cloudspeak | 2005

CLOSED: 4 X 4 X 2 INCHES (10.2 X 10.2 X 5 CM)

Denim, abaca, cotton linter, kozo, recycled paper, colored fibers, thistle, waxed linen, leaves, acrylic; Greek binding; painted

PHOTO BY DAVID BRIGGS

Deena Schnitman

Untitled | 2005

6½ X 5 X 1½ INCHES (16.5 X 12.7 X 3.8 CM)

Handmade paste paper, acid-free textblock,
bookcloth, waxed linen; buttonhole stitched

PHOTO BY JEFF BAIRD

Nancy Callahan

Cauliflower: Heat Resistant Variety Makes a
Good Cauliflower Grower Out of Anyone | 1995

18 X 32 X 18 INCHES (45.7 X 81.3 X 45.7 CM)
Cloth, string, wire, burlap; screen printed
PHOTO BY ARTIST

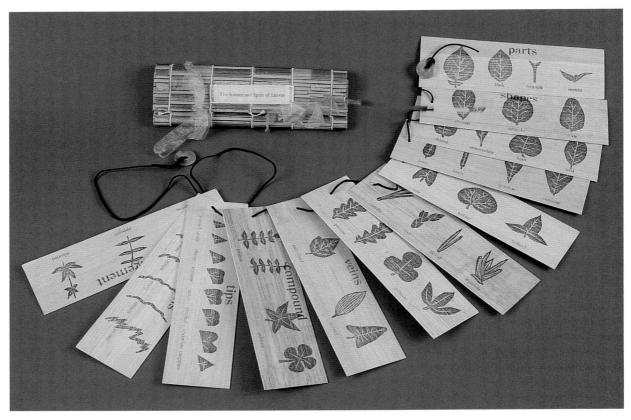

Catherine Alice Michaelis

The Science and the Spirit of Leaves | 2001

IN WRAPPER: 3¹/₂ X 9¹/₂ X 1 INCHES (8.9 X 24.1 X 2.5 CM);
CIRCLE DISPLAY: 27 X ¹/₁₆ INCHES (68.6 X 0.2 CM)

Veneer, cotton paper, leather cord, stone, bamboo, ribbon, silk;
palm leaf binding; painted, letterpress, linoleum printed; woven, sewn

PHOTO BY RICHARD NICOL

Peter Thomas
Donna Thomas

Paper from Plants | 1999

11 5/8 X 8 3/4 X 1 INCHES (29.5 X 22.2 X 2.5 CM)

Handmade paper, painted paperboards, Moroccan leather;
edition binding; letterpress; illustration by Donna Thomas

PHOTO BY ARTIST

Elizabeth Rotchford-Long

Mount Hope: Grave Thoughts | 2006

13 X 10 INCHES (33 X 25.4 CM)

Handmade lichen paper, printmaking paper; accordion binding; monoprint, gelatin printing, solvent transfers

PHOTOS BY D. J. EVANS

Andie Thrams

Time in the Trees (title page) | 2001–02

9 X 16¹/₂ X ³/₈ INCHES (22.9 X 41.9 X 1 CM)

Arches watercolor paper, linen thread, paste paper, gold leaf; Coptic binding, written, painted, drawn

PHOTO BY ARTIST

Teresa Childers

Falling Leaves: A Star Book | 2006

8 X 3³/₈ X 1¹/₂ INCHES (20.3 X 8.6 X 3.8 CM)
Canson Mi-Teintes paper, book board, ribbon,
embroidery floss; star book binding; hand cut
PHOTOS BY ARTIST

Gail Stiffe

Evolution | 2002

7⁷/₈ X 6¹¹/₁₆ X 1³/₄ INCHES (20 X 16.9 X 4.4 CM)

Cast handmade paper, paint, wax, bookcloth and book board; concertina binding; wraparound cover

PHOTO BY TIM GRESHAM

Charlotte Bird

Stitched Meditations | 2003

10 X 10½ X 1 INCHES (25.4 X 26.7 X 2.5 CM)

Silk dupioni, interfacing, cotton, metallic and linen thread, binder board, textile paint, silk frog; machine sewn, silkscreened, embroidered

PHOTOS BY JACK YONN

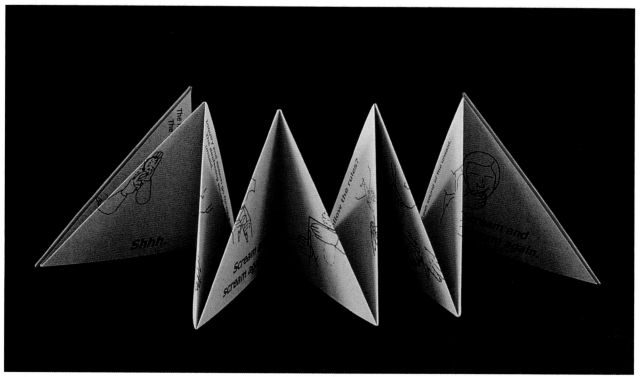

Judith E. Christensen
Scream and Scream Again | 1999

4 X 4 X ½ INCHES (10.2 X 10.2 X 1.3 CM)
Canson Mi-Teintes, Fabriano Ingres papers, hard covers;
accordion binding; photocopy transfer, digital printing
PHOTOS BY ARTIST

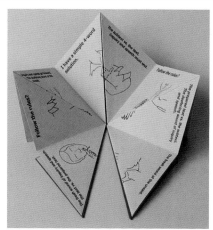

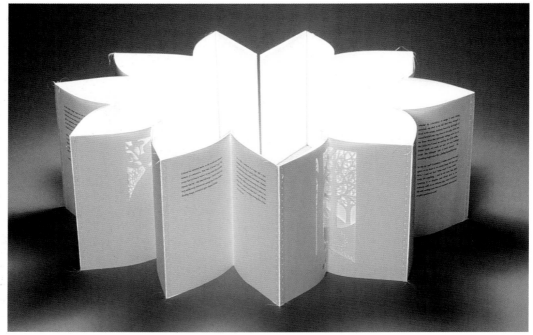

Katy Locke

A Winter's Walk | 2006

CLOSED: 11 X 7 X ¾ INCHES (27.9 X 17.8 X 1.9 CM);
OPEN: 11 X 28 INCHES (27.9 X 71.1 CM)

Rice paper, bookbinders board, vellum,
organdy ribbon, rayon thread; accordion binding;
hand-cut, layered paper

PHOTOS BY AL KAREVY

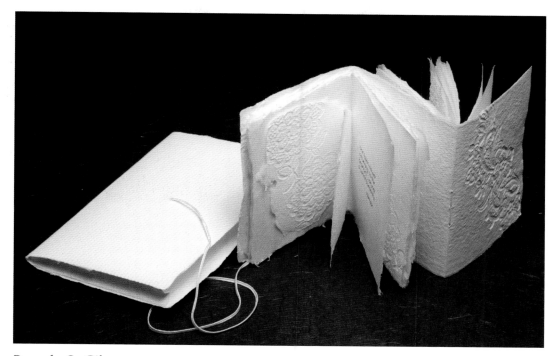

Pamela S. Gibson

White Butterfly | 2004

6 X 4½ X ½ INCHES (15.2 X 11.4 X 1.3 CM)

Abaca, cotton, kozo and handmade paper; dos-a-dos
binding; wet embossed, Gocco printed

PHOTO BY JAMES DERY

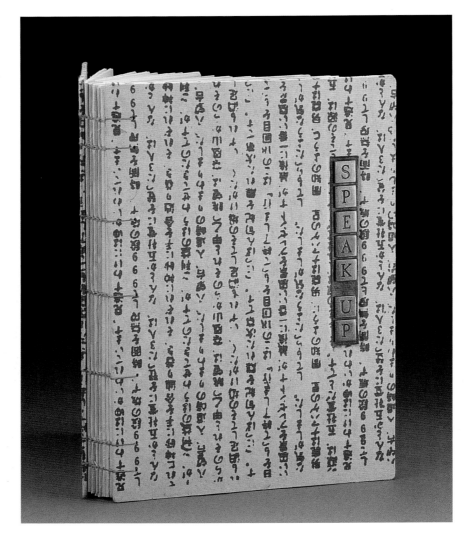

Bryony A. Smith

Free Speech | 2006

9¹⁄₄ X 6¹⁄₄ X ³⁄₄ INCHES (23.5 X 15.9 X 1.9 CM)

Nepali Lokta paper, brass letters, white sulfite text paper,
waxed linen thread; single-needle Coptic stitch; inkjet printed

PHOTO BY TOM MILLS

Elsie Sampson

Chinese Kitchen | 2005

9 X 6 X 1 INCHES (22.9 X 15.2 X 2.5 CM)

Manila envelope, elastic band, chopstick, beeswax, matchstick, feather, Chinese lucky money packet, beads, sequins, used coffee filter, bottlecap, cupcake lining, doll, Chinese newspaper, joss paper, raffia, kitchen-related ephemera; photocopied

PHOTOS BY HOWARD GOODMAN

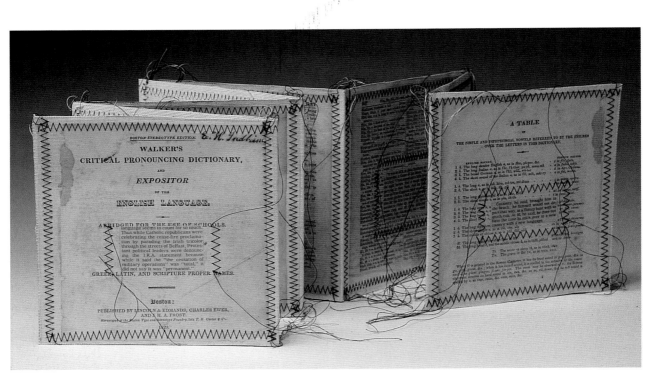

Patricia Malarcher
Word Web | 2004

6 X 6 X ½ INCHES (15.2 X 15.2 X 1.3 CM)

Dictionary pages, newspaper text, acetate,
canvas, thread; machine stitching

PHOTO BY D. JAMES DEE

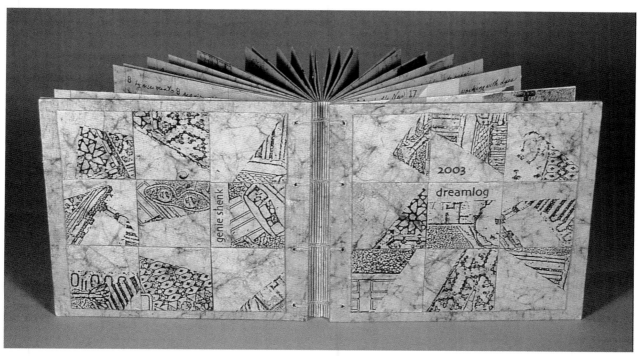

Genie Shenk

Dreaming 2003 | 2003–04

CLOSED: 5 X 5¼ X 1 INCHES (12.7 X 13.3 X 2.5 CM)

Batik paper, ink; Coptic binding; transfer print, collage

PHOTOS BY ARTIST

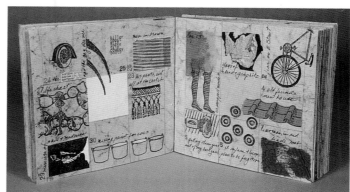

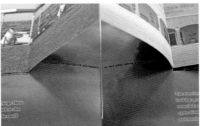

Philip B. Zimmermann

Shelter | 2006

11 X 8 1/2 X 1/2 INCHES (27.9 X 21.6 X 1.3 CM)
Hahnemühle rag paper, board covers; hand
bound with link stitch; archival inkjet printed

PHOTOS BY ARTIST

Dorothy A. Yule

Souvenirs of Great Cities (New York, Paris, London, San Francisco) | 1996

BOOKS: 2 X 2 X ³/₄ INCHES (5 X 5 X 1.9 CM) EACH; BOX: 5¹/₂ X 5¹/₂ X ⁷/₈ INCHES (14 X 14 X 2.2 CM)

Mohawk Superfine cover; double-sided concertina binding, pop-ups, removable spines; letterpress, hand cut and assembled; illustrations by Susan Hunt Yule

PHOTO BY ARTIST

Rosemary Kate Jesionowski

Greetings from Bloomington, Indiana | 2004

½ X 8¼ X ⅛ INCHES (8.9 X 21 X 0.3 CM)

Postcards, photographs; assembled; inkjet printed

PHOTOS BY ARTIST

Diane Cassidy

The Train Book | 2001

GAME BOARD, CLOSED: 9 X 12 X 1 INCHES (22.9 X 30.5 X 2.5 CM);
OPEN: 18 X 24 INCHES (45.7 X 61 CM); TRAIN: 62 INCHES (157.5 CM)

Game board, Tyvek, train cars, cardstock, paper, washers,
nails, original photos, accordion-style hinge; drawn, painted

PHOTO BY ARTIST

Sara G.H. Owen
Visiting Green Mountain | 2006

6 X 9 INCHES (15.2 X 22.9 CM)

Mohawk cover stock, Rives heavyweight, linen
thread; pamphlet stitch; color reduction print,
linoleum block, letterpress, handset metal type

PHOTOS BY TERESA GOLSON

Karen Koshgarian

September 11—A Memorial | 2005

6 X 2½ X ½ INCHES (15.2 X 6.4 X 1.3 CM)

Original photographs, news photographs; altered book

PHOTO BY ARTIST

Charles Hobson

Dancing with Amelia | 2000

8³/₄ X 6¹/₂ X 1¹/₄ INCHES (22.2 X 16.5 X 3.2 CM)

Laser-cut boards, cloth; accordion binding; Iris printed

PHOTOS BY ARTIST

Bonnie O'Connell

River Roll: American River Names | 2002

CLOSED: 4½ X 6½ X 1½ INCHES (11.4 X 16.5 X 3.8 CM)

Vintage postcards, transparencies, bookcloth, binders board, brass tubing; concertina binding

PHOTOS BY LARRY GAWELL

Barbara Michener

Immersed | 2006

CLOSED: 1³/₄ X 4¹/₂ X 6 INCHES (4.4 X 11.4 X 15.2 CM)

Plywood, watercolor paper, goat leather, button, encaustic

PHOTOS BY ARTIST

Pamela Paulsrud
Book Stones | 2000–06

AVERAGE SIZE: 2 X 2½ X 1 INCHES (5.1 X 6.4 X 2.5 CM)
Altered books, stones
PHOTO BY ARTIST

Christina Seely

Reservoir | 2005

9 X 6 X 1 INCHES (22.9 X 15.2 X 2.5 CM)
Paper; perfect bound; digital printing
PHOTO BY ARTIST

Betsy Kruger

Manzanita | 2006

7³/₄ X 22 X ¹/₂ INCHES (19.7 X 55.9 X 1.3 CM)

Somerset paper, commercial handmade paper, binders
board; Concertina binding, flag book; inkjet printed

PHOTO BY ARTIST

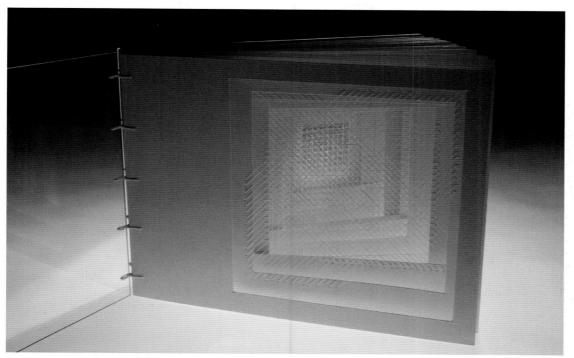

Adèle Outteridge

Between the Lines (White) | 2005

CLOSED: 8 X 10³⁄₄ X 1¹⁄₂ INCHES (20.3 X 27.3 X 3.8 CM)

Paper, Perspex, linen thread

PHOTOS BY DOUG SPOWART

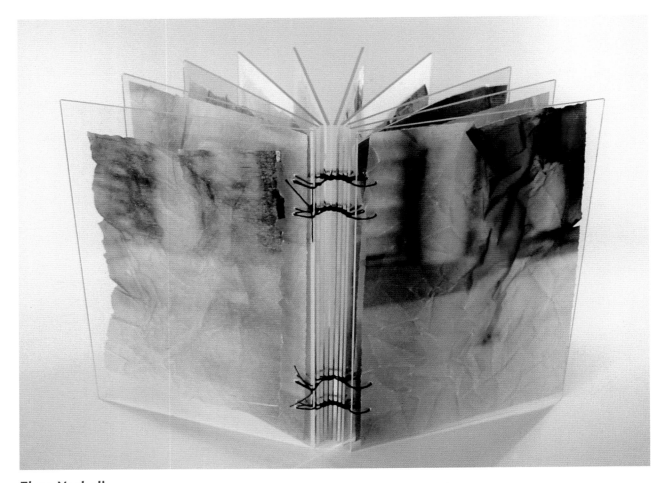

Elysa Voshell

The Inner Lives of Fleeting Shadows | 2004

8¹⁄₄ X 5³⁄₄ X 2 INCHES (21 X 14.6 X 5 CM)

Vegetable parchment, acrylic; Coptic binding; molded, inkjet printed

PHOTO BY ARTIST

Melissa Kaup-Augustine

Ele-Mental | 2006

5¹/₂ X 5¹/₂ X ³/₈ INCHES (14 X 14 X 1 CM)

Canson Johannot mold-made paper; accordion
fold with wrap cover; letterpress, vintage wood
type and modern polymer plates

PHOTOS BY KATE GODFREY

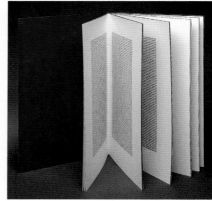

Peter Koch
Ur-Text Volume III | 1994

16 X 10½ X 1 INCHES (40.6 X 26.7 X 2.5 CM)

Mohawk Superfine paper, acid-etched zinc, brass, braided Dacron thread, aluminum, various metals; hand bound by Daniel Kelm, letterpress

PHOTOS BY ARTIST

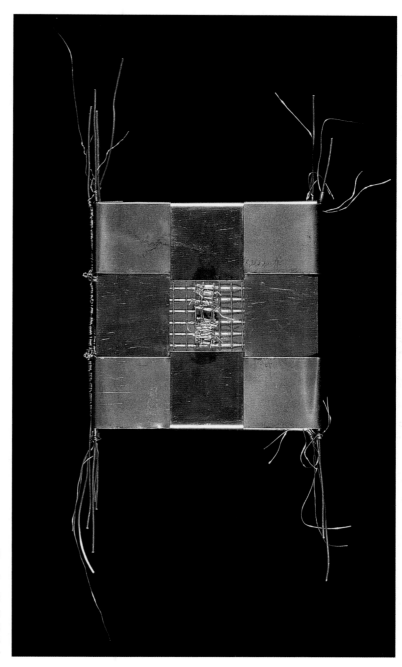

Alice M. Vinson

Keep Out | 2003

15 X 5 X 1 INCHES (38.1 X 12.7 X 2.5 CM)

Aluminum wire, steel, aluminum;
codex binding, unique wire binding;
black-and-white photographs

PHOTO BY ARTIST

Alicia Bailey

Antropa Mandragora | 2003

CLOSED: 10 X 4 X 1 INCHES (25.4 X 10.2 X 2.5 CM)

Glue chip glass; Coptic single-sheet binding; stained, painted, fired

PHOTO BY ARTIST

Charlene H. Matthews

Abecedarium | 1998

8 1/8 X 8 3/4 X 3/4 INCHES (20.6 X 22.2 X 1.9 CM)

Lenticles, paste-paper letters, silver leather spine, buckles; sewn

PHOTOS BY DEBORAH ROUNDTREE

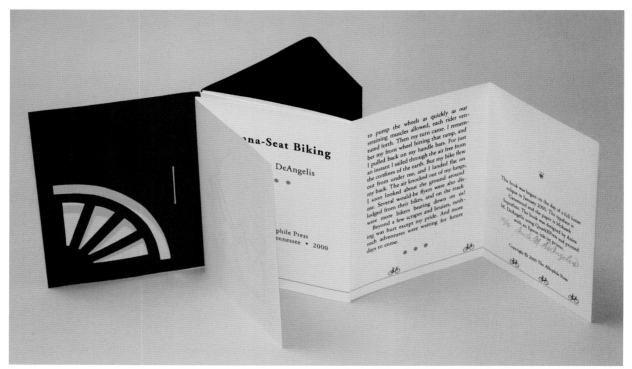

Anita M. DeAngelis

Banana-Seat Biking | 2000

4¼ X 3⅜ X ⅛ INCHES (10.7 X 8.5 X 0.3 CM)

Paper; modified Origami fold,
wraparound cover; inkjet printed

PHOTOS BY ARTIST

Anna Marie Ottaviano

Wanna Play? | 2004

10¹/₄ X 19¹/₄ X ¹/₂ INCHES (26 X 48.9 X 1.3 CM)

Somerset paper, book board, bookcloth, black cotton thread; stab binding; intaglio, lithography

PHOTOS BY ARTIST

THREE CAGES

a studio without windows
is a cell a haven
this basement space
its double doored stairwell
leading down

Joyce Arlene Cutler-Shaw
Three Cages | 1992

CLOSED: 4¹/₈ X 8¹/₄ INCHES (10.5 X 21 CM)
Cotton paper; angular fan fold, triangular fold;
letterpress, hand assembled
PHOTO BY PHEL STEINMETZ

Michael A. Henninger

The Book of Love | 2005–06

7½ X 13 X 6/10 INCHES (19 X 33 X 1.5 CM)

Canvas, paper, bronze, linen thread; sewn signatures,
gate-fold structure; cast bronze, digital printing

PHOTOS BY ARTIST

Judith I. Serebrin
Worry Book I | 1992

7 X 5 X 1 INCHES (17.8 X 12.7 X 2.5 CM)
Rives BFK, ink, clear plastic sheeting, paper;
folded monotypes; offset lithography; sewn, etched
PHOTO BY ARTIST

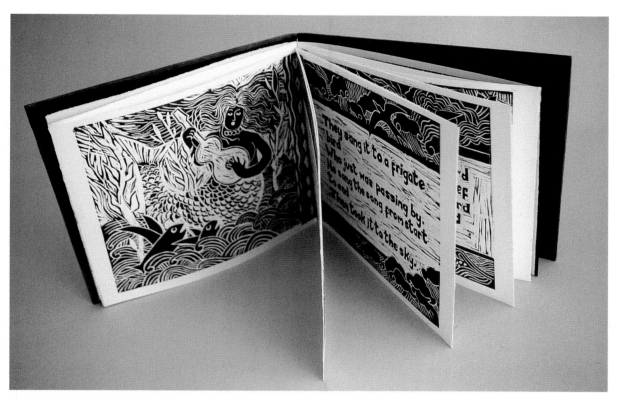

Frances Watson

How We Lost the Mermaid's Song | 2006

CLOSED: 9³⁄₄ X 11 ¹⁄₂ INCHES (24.7 X 29.2 CM);
OPEN: 9³⁄₄ X 23 ¹⁄₂ INCHES (24.7 X 59.7 CM)

Davey Board, Rives Heavy paper;
accordion binding; linocut, hinged

PHOTOS BY ARTIST

Mary Howe
Wasps as Paper Makers | 2003

3 X 3½ X 3½ INCHES (7.6 X 8.9 X 8.9 CM)

Handmade paper, bookcloth, wasp nest, mica, box; accordion binding

PHOTOS BY KEN WOISARD

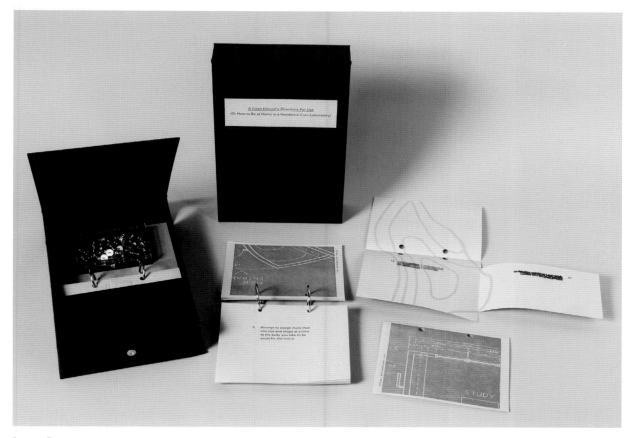

Inge Bruggeman

A Crisis Ethicist's Directions for Use | 2003

10 X 6½ X 2 INCHES (25.4 X 16.5 X 5.1 CM)

Handmade paper, bookcloth, plastic box, thumbtacks;
metal ring binding; single-tray box with clasp, letterpress,
photopolymer plates, handset type

PHOTO BY BILL MORRISON

Julie Chen

Personal Paradigms: A Game of Human Experience | 2003

15½ X 11¼ X 4¾ INCHES (39.4 X 28.6 X 12.1 CM)

Various papers, folding game board, instruction booklet, spinner, die, metal arrows, wooden spinner, game pieces, clear plastic sheeting, paper, cloth, resin; letterpress, photopolymer plates

PHOTOS BY SIBILA SAVAGE

Diane Cassidy

The Ten Plagues of Egypt | 2001

BOX, CLOSED: 7 X 11 X 22 INCHES (17.8 X 27.9 X 55.9 CM);
BOX, OPEN: 18 X 11 X 11 INCHES (45.7 X 27.9 X 27.9 CM);
SCROLL: 10 X 100 INCHES (25.4 X 254 CM)

Old ammunitions box, mulberry paper scroll,
sewing spools, back lighting; tacket binding;
stamped, scanned images

PHOTOS BY ARTIST

Bea Nettles

Deer Isle, Maine | 2002

5 X 3¾ X 1¼ INCHES (12.7 X 9.5 X 3.2 CM)

Leather, papyrus, artist paper, linen thread, colored pencil, walnut ink, brass pegs; Coptic binding; etched, cyanotype, silver gelatin prints, handwritten text, hand-carved bone

PHOTOS BY GAVIN SUNTOP

Jackie Niemi

Evolution | 2004

5 X 6¼ X 1 INCHES (12.7 X 15.9 X 2.5 CM)

Paper, linen thread, plant materials, walnut and oak gall inks,
clay pigment, foam core, museum board; tacket binding;
collage, stitched, stamped, written, painted

PHOTO BY ARTIST

Nancy Overton

Untitled | 2005

5 1/2 X 4 1/4 X 1 INCHES (14 X 10.8 X 2.5 CM)
Calf leather, waxed linen thread;
long stitch and weave stitch; hand dyed
PHOTOS BY ARTIST

Molly Irene Brauhn

Content of Disaster | 2002

11 X 10 X ½ INCHES (27.9 X 25.4 X 1.3 CM)

BFK Rives; Japanese side stitch; soaked, stained, silkscreened, stone lithography

PHOTO BY ARTIST

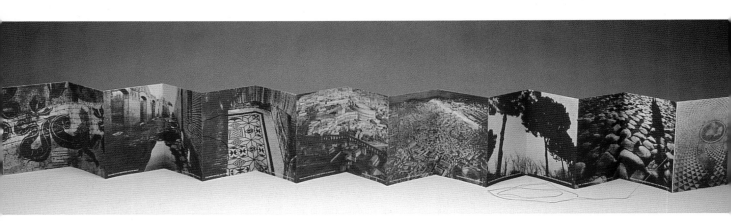

Cynthia Lollis
Daniela Deeg

Relinquo | 2005

9¼ X 7¼ X 1 INCHES (2.5 X 18.4 X 2.5 CM)

Moriki paper, wood, wax, waxed thread,
grayboard box; accordion binding; screen printed

PHOTOS BY WALKER MONTGOMERY

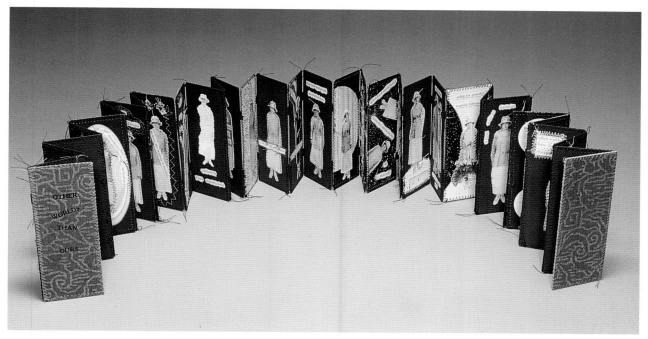

Lisa Kokin

Other Worlds Than Ours | 2002

CLOSED: 5 X 2 X 2¹/₄ INCHES (12.7 X 5 X 5.7 CM)

Found text and photos, thread, paper, photo cardboard;
accordion binding; machine stitched, sewn

PHOTO BY JOHN WILSON WHITE

Nancy Pobanz

Standing Ground | 2003

6 X 5¾ X 1 INCHES (15.2 X 14.6 X 2.5 CM)

Watercolor paper, acrylic ink, marker, linen tape; sewn signatures; handwritten, collage

PHOTOS BY LIGHTWORKS PHOTOGRAPHY

Mary Ellen Long

Pagings | 1998

6 X 5½ X 5 INCHES (15.2 X 14 X 12.7 CM)

Arches paper, copper, nature-altered book pages, linen thread; accordion binding, running stitch attachment; hand stamped, collage

PHOTO BY ARTIST

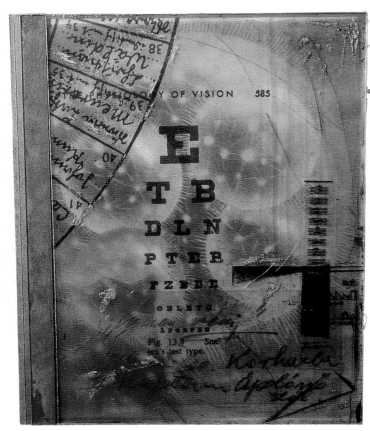

Dan Mayer

Shrift/Werk | 2004

CLOSED: 6 X 4 X ¼ INCHES (15.2 X 10.2 X 0.6 CM)

Lazertran images, gold leaf; origami,
collograph, collage, drawn, lithography

PHOTOS BY ARTIST

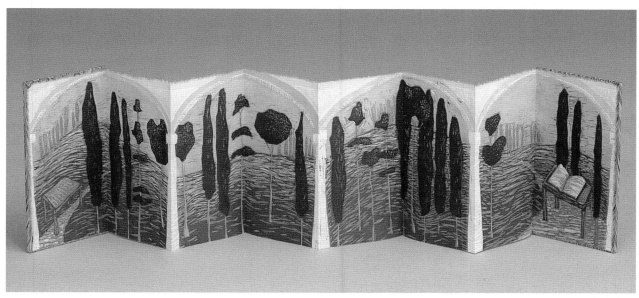

Jenni Freidman
Finding Florence | 2001

5 1/2 X 3 3/4 X 1/4 INCHES (14 X 9.5 X 0.6 CM)
Japanese paper, Italian hand-marbled paper;
accordion binding; letterpress, woodcut

PHOTOS BY LARRY GAWEL

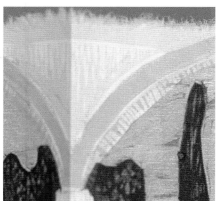

Crystal Cawley

44 Brains | 2003

3 X 2½ X 2½ INCHES (7.6 X 6.4 X 6.4 CM)

Various papers, leather, ceramic covers, found objects, thread, copper and brass wire, acrylic; glued page spreads; watercolor, embroidery

PHOTOS BY JAY YORK

Crystal Cawley

Backbone: Theme and Variations | 2005

8½ X 3 X 3½ INCHES (21.6 X 7.6 X 8.9 CM)
Reclaimed book parts, found objects, graphite,
wire; accordion binding; collage, print transfer

PHOTOS BY JAY YORK

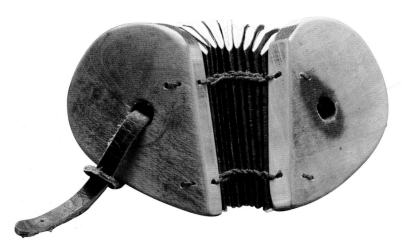

Melissa Sullivan

Lesson Learned | 2004

CLOSED: 2 X 1³/₄ X 1¹/₈ INCHES (5 X 4.4 X 2.8 CM)

Ingres and Cave papers, waxed linen, fruitwood leather; coptic binding

PHOTO BY ARTIST

Diane Bond

Strap Bound Journal | 1993

3 X 4¹/₂ X 1³/₄ INCHES (7.6 X 11.4 X 4.4 CM)

Text weight paper, bookcloth, binders board, vintage Asian wallpaper sample, leaves, grass cloth, jeweler's cord

PHOTO BY PAUL BOND

Erin Ciulla

Piano Piano | 2006

4 X 4 X 2 INCHES (10.2 X 10.2 X 5 CM) EACH

Crocheted covers, linen, mohair, wool,
handmade cotton paper; long stitch binding

PHOTO BY ROBIN TIEU

Amy Pirkle

Untitled | 2006

9¹⁄₈ X 6¹⁄₄ X 2³⁄₈ INCHES (23.2 X 15.9 X 6 CM)

Wooden boards, Nigerian goat leather, Mohawk text weight paper, linen thread, brass clasps; Byzantine binding; blind tooling

PHOTOS BY TERESA GOLSON

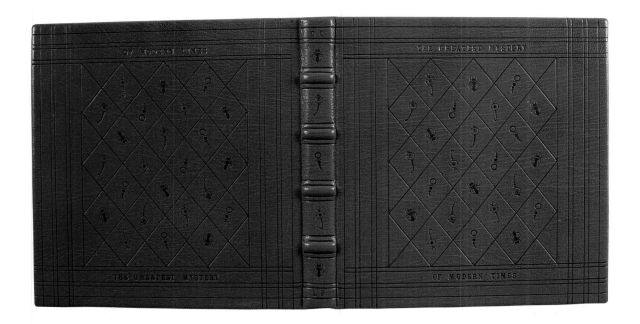

Scott Kellar

Crop Circles: The Greatest Mystery of Modern Times by Lucy Pringle | 2002

9 X 11 ½ X 1 INCHES (22.9 X 29.2 X 2.5 CM)

Terra-cotta goatskin; medieval-style blind tooling

PHOTO BY ARTIST

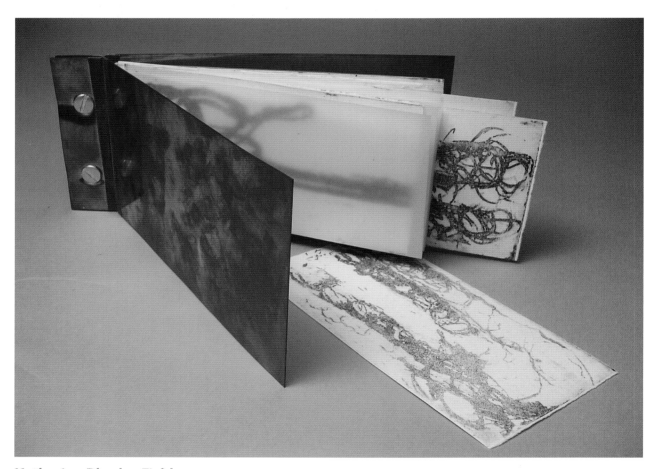

Katherine Rhodes Fields

Knots | 2005

3 1/2 X 8 X 1/2 INCHES (8.9 X 20.3 X 1.3 CM)
Rives BFK, vellum, bookcloth, copper flashing;
screw post; copper plate etchings
PHOTO BY ARTIST

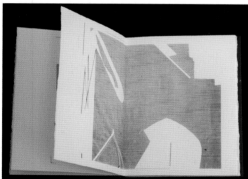

Roberta Lavadour

Remains | 2005

7½ X 5½ X ½ INCHES (19 X 14 X 1.3 CM)
Rives BFK, bookcloth; drum leaf binding;
laser printed, foil stamped
PHOTOS BY ARTIST

Camille Winer

Sweet Compulsions: Assorted Affairs | 2003

11 X 6½ X 2 INCHES (27.9 X 16.5 X 5 CM)

Momigami and Stonehenge papers; book-board construction; inkjet printed

PHOTOS BY EDWARD DANIEL

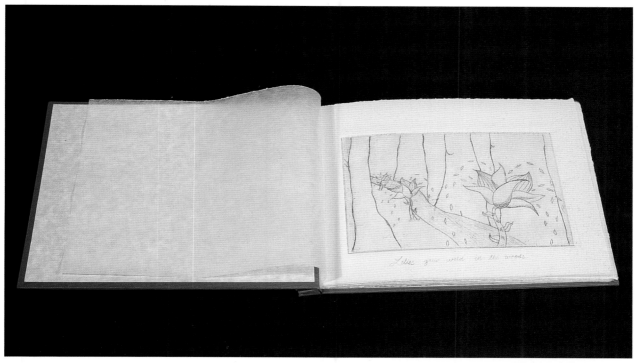

Alexis Adams

History Book | 2005

5 X 7 X ½ INCHES (12.7 X 17.8 X 1.3 CM)

Rives BFK and Moriki papers; Japanese
stab binding; drypoint intaglio, cyanotype

PHOTOS BY ARTIST

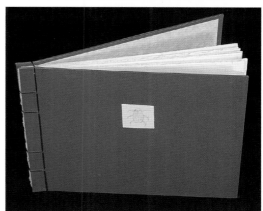

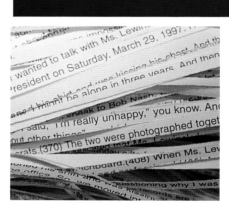

William Drendel

The Starr Report: Beat Yourself Up, America! | 1998

8 X 27 X 11 INCHES (20.3 X 68.6 X 27.9 CM)

Paper, dyed oak; laser printed

PHOTOS BY ARTIST

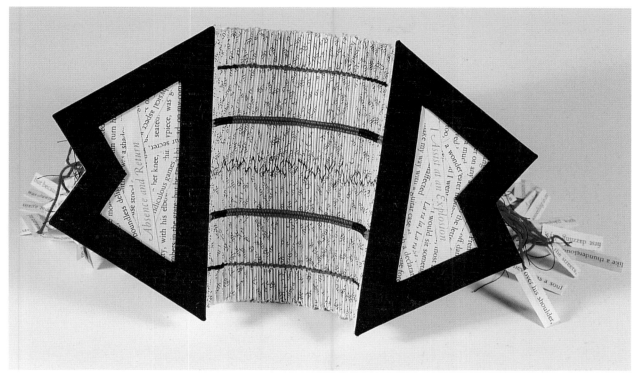

Bonnie O'Connell

Assist at an Explosion | 2005

6 X 8 X 5½ INCHES (15.2 X 20.3 X 14 CM)

Magazine pages, linen thread, reclaimed cord, binders
board, bookcloth; double raised cord binding

PHOTOS BY JEFF HALVIN

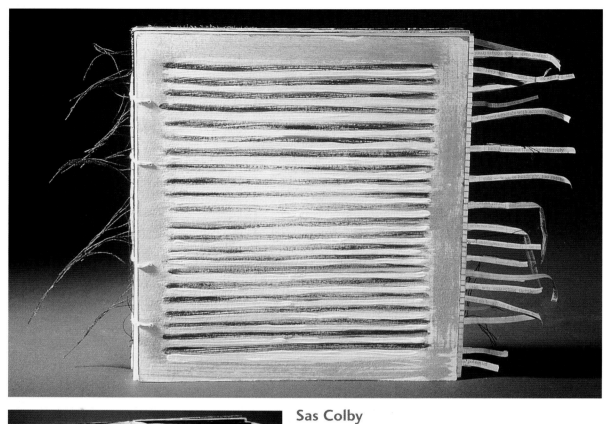

Sas Colby

Lines | 2004–05

8 X 7½ X ⅝ INCHES (20.3 X 19 X 1.6 CM)

Newspaper, gesso, textile, museum board;
Coptic binding; stitched, digital printing, collage

PHOTOS BY KATE CAMERON

Mary Howe

ABZ Bees | 2002

2¼ X 8 X 6¼ INCHES (5.7 X 20.3 X 15.9 CM)

Bookcloth, handmade paste papers, wire, silk thread, ink, colored pencil; Coptic binding, pop-up, pamphlet, flip book; collage

PHOTOS BY KEN WOISARD

Jeanne Germani

Wings | 2003

2½ X 3½ X 1¾ INCHES (6.4 X 8.9 X 4.4 CM)

Stonehenge paper, found paper, balsa wood, wings, antique necklace parts, metal cross and bird, thread; accordion flutter binding; collage, decorative stitching, photo transfer, blender pen transfer

PHOTO BY DAVID BRIGGS

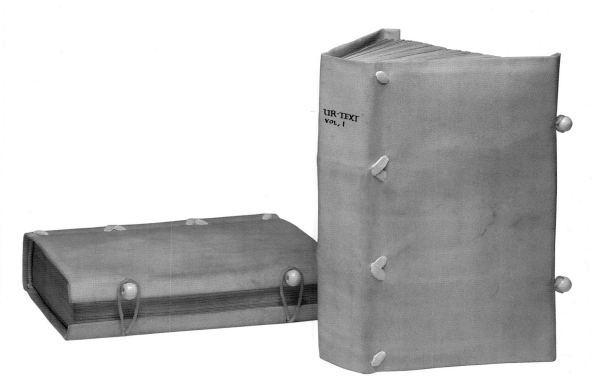

Peter Koch
Ur-Text Volume I | 1994

6½ X 4¼ X 1 INCHES (16.5 X 10.8 X 2.5 CM)

Serpa handmade paper, goatskin thongs, calfskin vellum, Tibetan bone bead clasps; hand bound by Daniel Flanagan; letterpress

PHOTOS BY ARTIST

Susan T. Viguers

The Universe Tends Toward Disorder | 2001

OPEN: 11 X 6½ X ³⁄₁₆ INCHES (27.9 X 16.5 X 0.5 CM)

Reclaimed wood shutters, Tyvek, Elephant Hide paper;
Jacob's Ladder structure; letterpress, screen printed

PHOTOS BY ARTIST

Jane De Haan
Willow | 2003

7½ X 7 X 1 INCHES (19 X 17.8 X 2.5 CM)
Handmade papers, bark, willow, waxed linen
PHOTOS BY GRACE WESTON

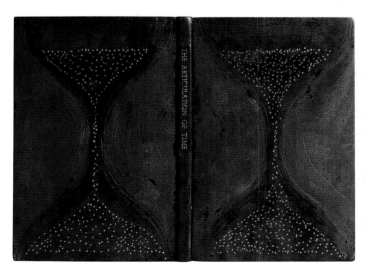

Don Taylor
The Articulation of Time | 2003

9³⁄₈ X 6³⁄₈ X ½ INCHES (23 X 16.2 X 1.3 CM)
Goatskin, gold leaf; blind tooling
PHOTO BY ARTIST

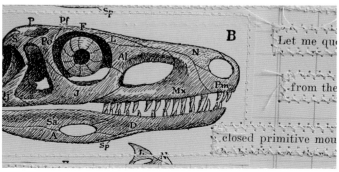

Lisa Kokin

The Origin of Birds | 1999

5½ X 2½ X 1 INCHES (14 X 6.4 X 2.5 CM)
Book spines, found text and images, thread;
machine stitched

PHOTOS BY JOHN WILSON WHITE

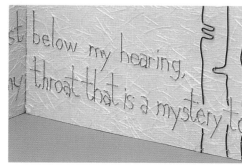

Artemis BonaDea

The Heart of the Birch Forest | 2006

CLOSED: 17³/₄ X 8¹/₂ X 1 INCHES (45.1 X 21.6 X 2.5 CM)

Fabric-covered paper, laminated paper,
wire, birch bark; assembled

PHOTOS BY FRANK FLAVIN

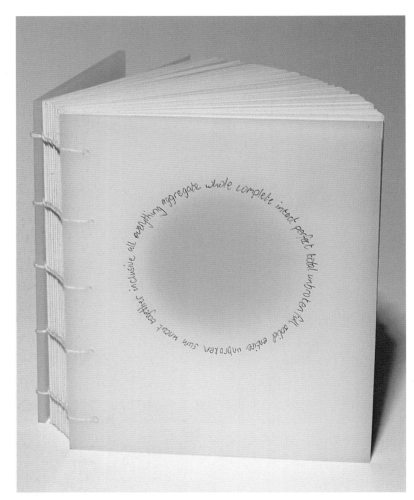

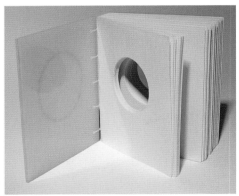

Susan Porteous

Whole | 2005

5 X 4¼ X 1¼ INCHES (12.7 X 10.8 X 3.2 CM)

Acrylic, paper; Coptic binding; handwritten text

PHOTOS BY ARTIST

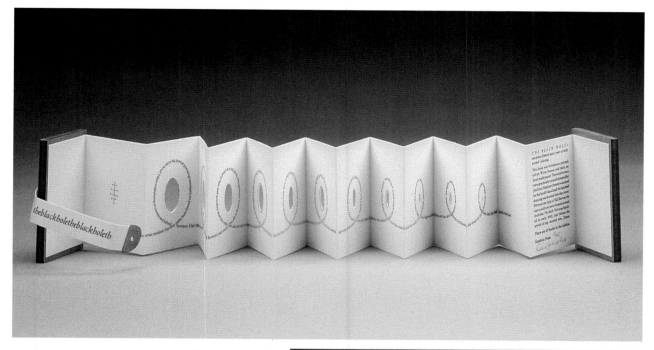

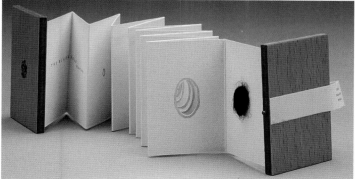

Diane Jacobs

The Black Hole | 2003

3 X 2 X ½ INCHES (7.6 X 5.1 X 1.3 CM)

Handmade paper, parchment strap, wooden covers,
human hairball; accordion binding; letterpress

PHOTOS BY BILL BACHHUBER

Mar Goman

Exhale | 2006

5½ X 3½ X 2 INCHES (14 X 8.9 X 5 CM)

Altered Moleskine notebook; Japanese-style binding;
mixed media, collage, sewn, drawn, painted, transfer

PHOTO BY BILL BACHUBER

Claudia Lee

Untitled | 1998

9 X 7 X ½ INCHES (22.9 X 17.8 X 1.3 CM)

Handmade and commercial papers, book board, waxed
linen, clay beads; stab binding; Gocco printing

PHOTO BY JOHN LUCAS

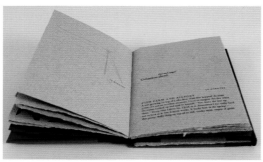

Ellen Knudson

*Self-Dual (How to Walk a
30,000-Mile Tightrope)* | 2006

4 X 6 INCHES (10.2 X 15.2 CM)

Handmade cotton and flax paper, Mingei dyed
paper, Iris bookcloth; built-in groove case binding,
dos-a-dos structure; letterpress, handset metal
types, linoleum reduction prints

PHOTOS BY MEGAN BEAN

Laurie Corral

Pulse | 2004

8 X 13¼ X ¾ INCHES (20.3 X 33.7 X 1.9 CM)
Arches cover, metal rods, dental floss, cloth;
sewn, woodcut, linocut, monoprint
PHOTO BY STEPHEN MANN

Katherine Nicholson

Engrams | 2005

5 X 6 X ½ INCHES (12.7 X 15.2 X 1.3 CM)

Accordion binding; collograph, letterpress, linoleum block prints

PHOTOS BY ARTIST

Inge Bruggeman

Simple Harmonic Motions | 2001

10¼ X 7½ X ½ INCHES (26 X 19 X 1.3 CM)

Kitakata paper, bookcloth; accordion binding;
letterpress, photocopy transfers

PHOTOS BY BILL MORRISON

Amy Pirkle

Daily Bread | 2006

6¼ X 4¾ X ¼ INCHES (15.9 X 12 X 0.6 CM)

Fabriano Ingres and Nideggen paper, linen thread; pamphlet binding, fold-out pages; letterpress

PHOTO BY TERESA GOLSON

Harriete Estel Berman

And There Was Light | 2004

14¼ X 9 X 3 INCHES (36.2 X 22.9 X 7.6 CM)

Reclaimed tin containers, vintage steel dollhouses, 10-karat gold and aluminum rivets, brass hinge pins, stainless steel screws, acrylic inks, gesso, hand-fabricated metal hinges; accordion binding; riveted

PHOTOS BY PHILIP COHEN

Mary Ann Sampson

Jazz | 2005

9³⁄₄ X 6³⁄₈ X ¹⁄₂ INCHES (24.7 X 16.2 X 1.3 CM)

Gold foil applied with heat, colored pencil;
Coptic binding; drawn, rubber stamped, cutouts

PHOTOS BY ARTIST

Sharon McCartney

Moonlight and Music | 2005

3¼ X 3¼ X ½ INCHES (8.3 X 8.3 X 1.3 CM)

Rice paper, vintage papers, stamps, thread, watercolor, acrylic; double flap page fold-outs; painted, drawn, photocopy transfer, gelatin printing, hand and machine stitched

PHOTO BY JOHN POLAK PHOTOGRAPHY

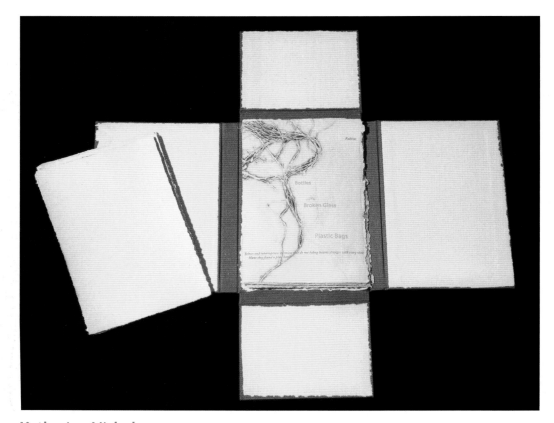

Katherine Nicholson

River Collections | 2006

6½ X 9½ X ¾ INCHES (16.5 X 24.1 X 1.9 CM)

Handmade saguaro paper, bookcloth; unbound portfolio;
collograph, letterpress, screen print

PHOTO BY MIKE LUNDGREN

Julie Chen

True to Life | 2004

TABLET: 9½ X 14¾ X 1 INCHES (24.1 X 37.5 X 2.5 CM);
BOX: 10 X 15 X 2½ INCHES (25.4 X 38.1 X 6.4 CM)

Various papers, bass wood, bookcloth, clear plastic sheeting;
tablet binding; letterpress, wood blocks, photopolymer plates

PHOTOS BY SIBILA SAVAGE

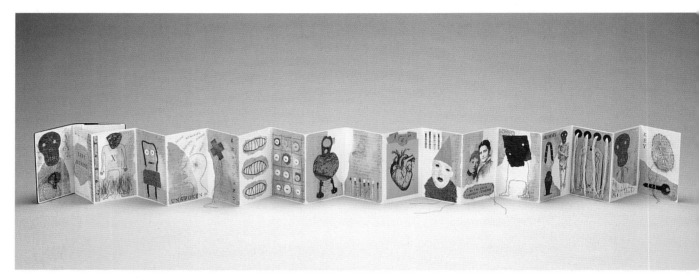

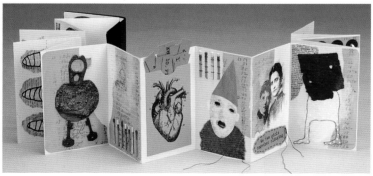

Mar Goman

Left Behind | 2006

CLOSED: 5½ X 3½ X 2 INCHES (14 X 8.9 X 5 CM)

Japanese-style Moleskine notebook, mixed media; collage, sewn, drawn, painted, transfer

PHOTOS BY BILL BACHUBER

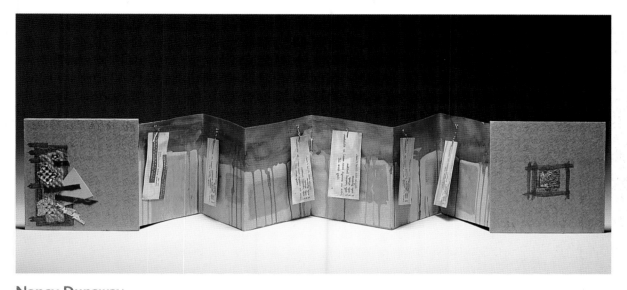

Nancy Dunaway

Feathers and Findings | 2003

OPEN: 5½ X 5½ X 36 INCHES (14 X 14 X 91.4 CM)

Mixed media, acrylic, graphite, feathers, found objects, metallic thread, metal; pocket concertina

PHOTO BY GEORGE CHAMBERS

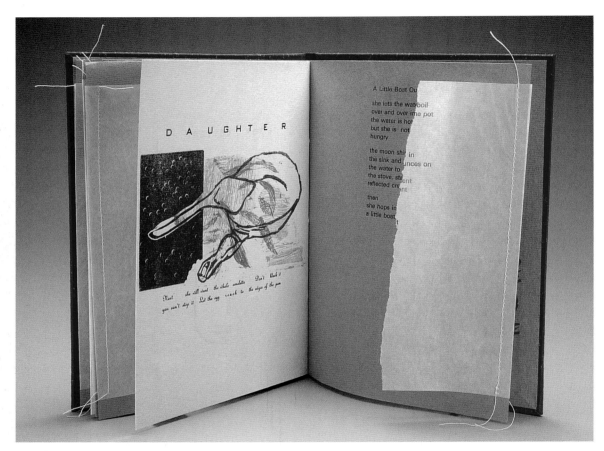

Alisa Golden

Steaming on the Stovetop: Poems from the Pantry | 2003

8¼ X 6⅛ INCHES (21 X 15.5 CM)

Museum board, glassine, thread, Asian papers, bookcloth;
single-signature binding; letterpress, linocut, collagraph

PHOTO BY SIBILA SAVAGE

Jeffrey Morin
Caren Heft

Martyr, Mercury, & Rooster | 2005

BOOKS: 12 X 9 X ½ INCHES (30.5 X 22.9 X 1.3 CM) EACH;
BOX: 13 X 10 X 2½ INCHES (33 X 25.4 X 6.4 CM)

Cotton, mica, linen tape, linen thread, wire, resistors, wire mesh, electric
couples, circuit board, copper leaf, pigment; Coptic binding on
concertina; letterpress, reduction linoleum blocks, photoengraving

PHOTOS COURTESY OF SEWANEE, THE UNIVERSITY OF THE SOUTH

Laura Wait

*X, Letter of Danger, Sex and the
Unknown, Vol. 1* | 2006

7³/₄ X 15³/₈ X ³/₄ INCHES (19.5 X 39 X 2 CM)

Leather, Cave and BFK papers, ink, paint; fine binding,
leather joints, sewn on concertina; letterpress,
collograph, hand tooled, painted, handwritten

PHOTOS BY ARTIST

Katrin Kapp Braun

Woman | 2005–2006

2¹⁵⁄₁₆ X 2¹⁵⁄₁₆ X 1³⁄₁₆ INCHES (7.5 X 7.5 X 3 CM)

Cotton abaca paper, Hahnemühle Biblio paper;
accordion binding; letterpress

PHOTO BY ARTIST

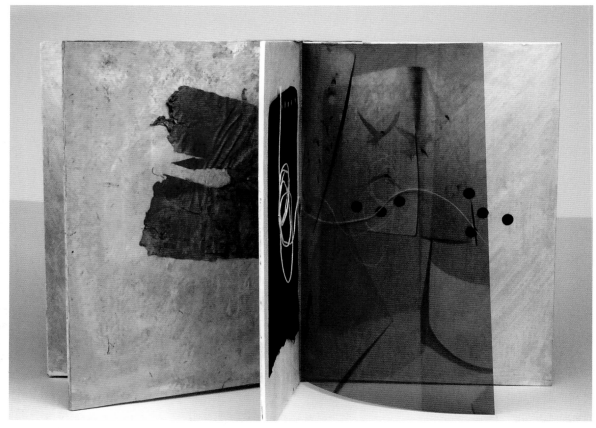

Arlyn Ende

Homage to Susan | 2006

8 X 12 X 1 INCHES (20.3 X 30.5 X 2.5 CM)

Gesso, book board, acrylic ink-tinted Tyvek, birch bark, Mylar, copper foil, linen threads, scanned images, handmade paper; scanned and cropped images, digital printing

PHOTOS BY JOSÉ BETANCOURT

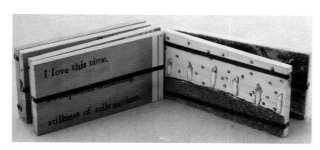

Lisa Beth Robinson

Nocturne | 2004

4⁷/₈ X 2³/₈ X 2¹/₄ INCHES (12.4 X 6.1 X 5.7 CM)

Mixed media, wood, steel shot, deer teeth,
star anise; Jacob's Ladder binding

PHOTOS BY ARTIST

Carolee Campbell

Burn Down the Zendo | 2004

5³/₄ X 15 X ¹/₄ INCHES (14.6 X 38.1 X 0.6 CM)

Handmade Egyptian tow flax paper, Japanese paper;
stab binding; letterpress, calligraphy

PHOTO BY ARTIST

Geraldine A. Newfry

Celadon Cicada | 2003

5¹/₂ X 4³/₄ X 2 INCHES (14 X 12.1 X 5 CM)

Mohawk superfine, handmade papers, polymer clay, found objects,
metal mesh, resin-encased cicada; long stitch; celadon technique

PHOTO BY LARRY SANDERS

Joy M. Campbell

3 in 1 Jacob's Ladder | 2005

4½ X 3¾ X 4½ INCHES (11.4 X 9.5 X 11.4 CM)

Book board, Japanese paper, grosgrain ribbons, bead, laminated cards, ladder, trick book; Jacob's Ladder construction for box; computer-generated text

PHOTOS BY JAMES HART

Stephen Murphy

Futhark | 2005

10 X 6 INCHES (25.4 X 15.2 CM)
Padauk wood, Sommerset paper; 8-needle Coptic stitch
binding; calligraphy, hand-carved title

PHOTOS BY ARTIST

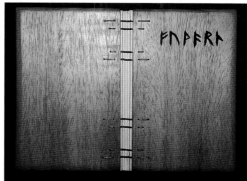

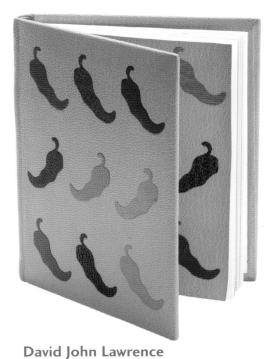

David John Lawrence
Hot Sauces | 2005

3³/₄ X 3¹/₈ X ¹/₂ INCHES (9.6 X 8 X 1.2 CM)
Goatskin, onlays, leather; fine binding
PHOTO BY BOBBY BADGER

Brian D. Cohen
The Bird Book | 2004

15³/₄ X 12 X 1³/₄ INCHES (40 X 30.5 X 4.4 CM)
Bird's-eye maple boards, leather hinges; open spine;
hand colored, relief etchings, letterpress
PHOTO BY ARTIST

Alice Austin

Bloom | 2006

7 X 8 X 1 INCHES (17.8 X 20.3 X 2.5 CM)

Paste paper, Rives heavyweight paper; accordion binding, central pop-up; monoprint, handset type

PHOTO BY ARTIST

Lesley Riley

Follow | 2005

9 X 9 X 1 INCHES (22.9 X 22.9 X 2.5 CM)

Lutradur, acrylics, fabrics, trims, vintage apparel, fusible interfacing, beads; sewn tab bindings; etched, machine stitched

PHOTOS BY ARTIST

Laura Russell

Simplify | 2004

OPEN: 5 1/2 X 5 1/2 X 42 INCHES (14 X 14 X 106.7 CM)

Leather, handmade paper; collage, printed

PHOTOS BY ARTIST

Martin Degn Pedersen

Henry Miller Breve til Anäis Nin
(Letters for Anäis Nin) | 1993

8¹⁄₄ X 6¹⁄₂ X 1¹⁄₄ INCHES (21 X 16.5 X 3 CM)

Goat leather, silk thread, gold; paper covertures;
French half binding; hand sewn

PHOTOS BY ARTIST

Julie Friedman

Tan Lines | 2004

CLOSED: 5 1/4 X 4 INCHES (13.3 X 10.2 CM)

Bristol board; monoprint, linocut,
copy transfer, rubber stamped

PHOTOS BY ARTIST

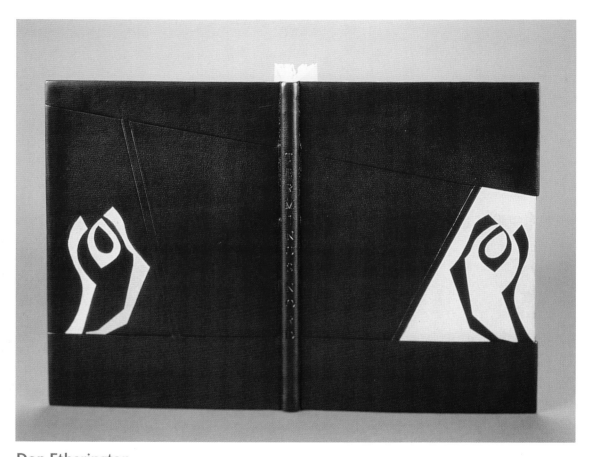

Don Etherington

Terminus Nord *by Genevieve Letarte,*
Illustrated by Louis-Pierre Bougire | 1996

14¼ X 11 X ¾ INCHES (36.2 X 27.9 X 1.9 CM)
Goatskin leather, vellum onlay; blind tooling, embroidered
PHOTO BY TIM BARKLEY

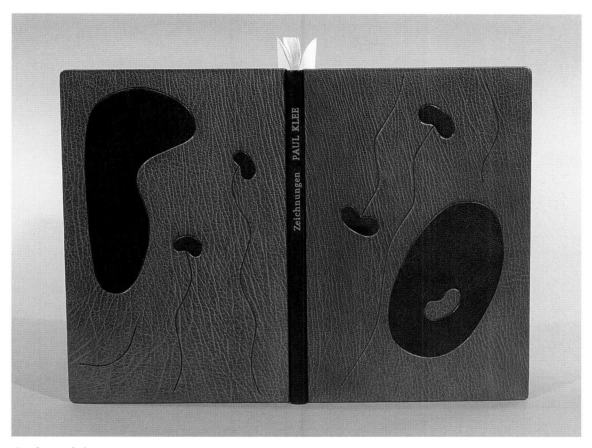

Cathy Adelman

Zeichnungen Paul Klee | 2003

9¹/₂ X 6¹/₄ X ¹⁵/₁₆ INCHES (24.1 X 15.9 X 1 CM)

Leather, onlays; three-piece binding; blind tooling

PHOTO BY STEVE COHEN

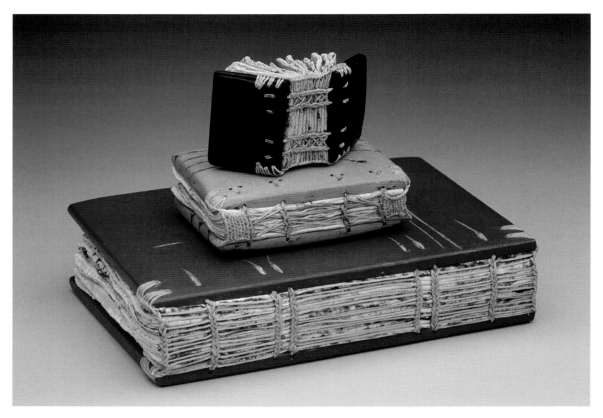

Shanna Leino

3 Sewn Books | 2005

1 ½ X 1 ¼ X 1 INCHES (3.8 X 3.2 X 2.5 CM);
3 ½ X 2 ¼ X ¾ INCHES (8.9 X 5.7 X 1.9 CM);
6 X 4 X 1 ¼ INCHES (15.2 X 10.2 X 3.2 CM)

Ebony, painted cedar, linen thread, silk and hemp cloth;
Coptic binding, band stitched; monoprint

PHOTO BY WALKER MONTGOMERY

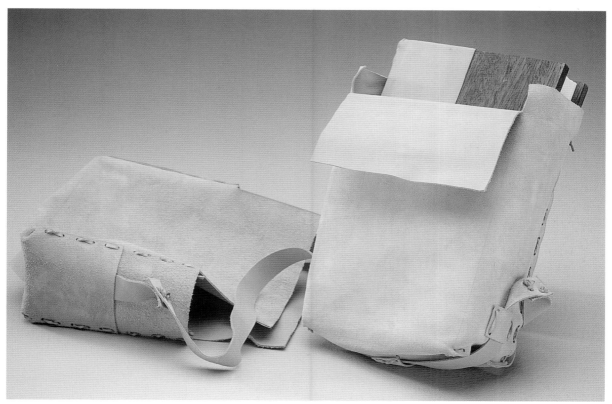

Marie C. Oedel

Ethiopian Book Bag | 2002

7½ X 5½ X 2¾ INCHES (19 X 14 X 7 CM) IN BOOK BAG
Mohawk Vellum, leather, wood, linen, thread;
conservation binding; sewn

PHOTOS BY DEAN POWELL

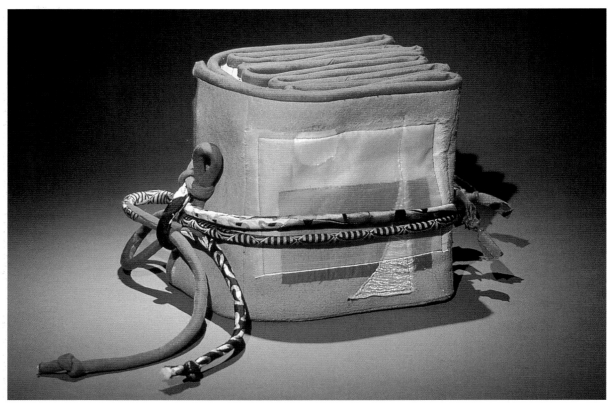

Susanne C. Scott

Book of Books | 2005

OPEN, WITH CORD: 85½ X 8 INCHES (217 X 30.5 CM)
Silk cotton, metal synthetics; accordion binding,
hand and machine stitched
PHOTOS BY JIM FERREIRA

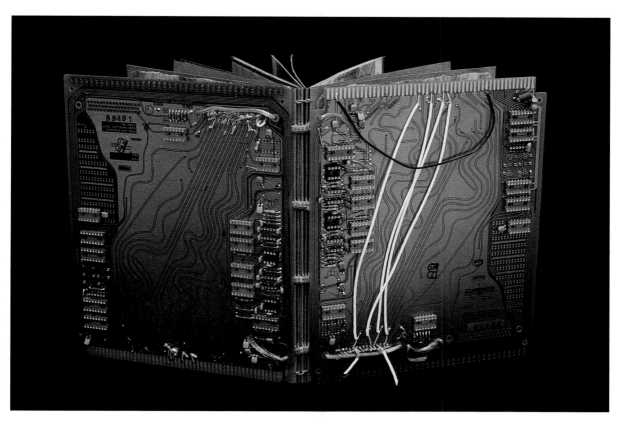

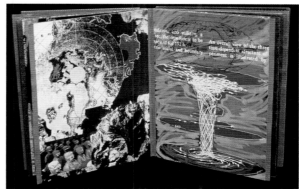

Paula Jull

And Now, Your Local Forecast | 2001

9 X 10 X ³/₄ INCHES (22.9 X 25.4 X 1.9 CM)

Computer circuit boards, handmade paper; inkjet printed

PHOTOS BY ISU PHOTO SERVICES

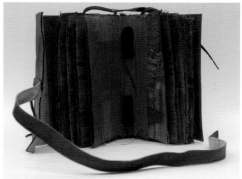

Dorothy Simpson Krause

Magdalene Laundries | 2003

6 X 4¼ X 1¼ INCHES (15.2 X 10.8 X 3.2 CM)

Reeves BFK, papyrus, leather and leather
inlays, mixed media; Coptic binding; collage

PHOTOS BY ARTIST

Rachel Melis

Seed Mix | 2004

1 X 2 X ¼ – 3 X 3 X ¼ INCHES (2.5 X 5 X 0.6 – 7 X 7.6 X 0.6 CM)

Paper, linen thread, linen cord, beeswax; letterpress, dipped, burned

PHOTO BY ARTIST

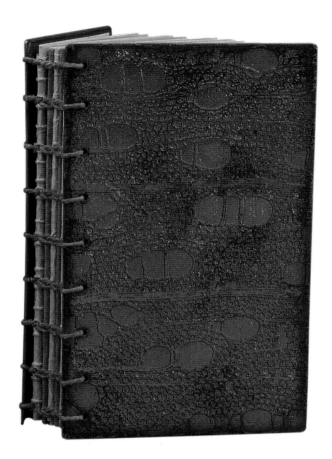

Amy Jacobs

Green Birchwood | 2004

4 1/2 X 2 1/2 X 3/4 INCHES (11.4 X 6.4 X 1.9 CM)

Enamel, copper, handmade flax paper, commercial paper, waxed linen thread; Coptic binding; etched

PHOTO BY TOM MILLS

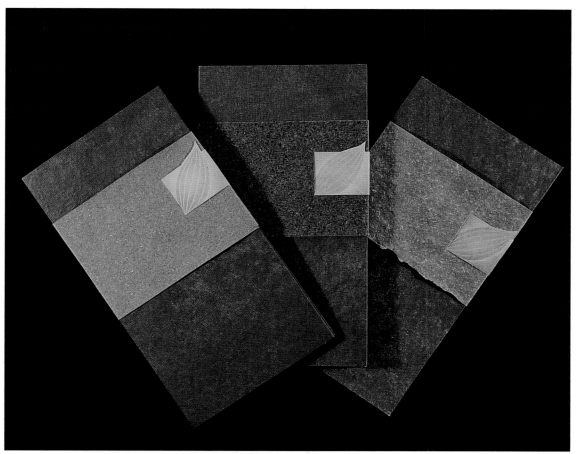

Melodie Carr

Will Grow Under Beeches | 1999

7 X 3³/₄ X ³/₁₆ INCHES (17.8 X 9.5 X 0.5 CM)

Handmade Alabama kozo and linen papers, paste paper; hand flourished, stenciled, letterpress

PHOTOS BY ARTIST

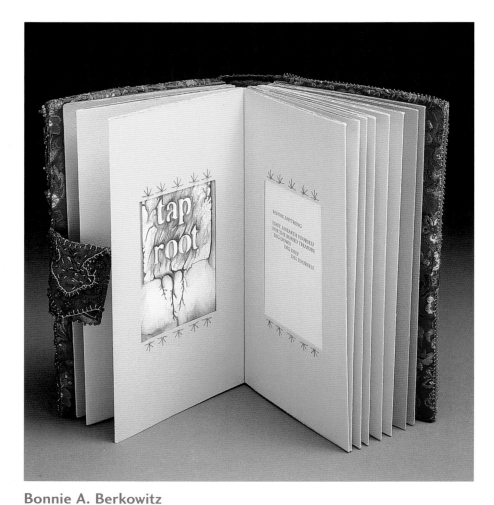

Bonnie A. Berkowitz

Tap Root: Stories from the Earth | 2005

8 X 5½ X 2¼ INCHES (20.3 X 14 X 5.7 CM)

Canson paper, cotton, silk thread, glass beads, gold thread;
double-sided accordion fold with pocket; drawn, embroidered

PHOTO BY CRAIG PHILLIPS

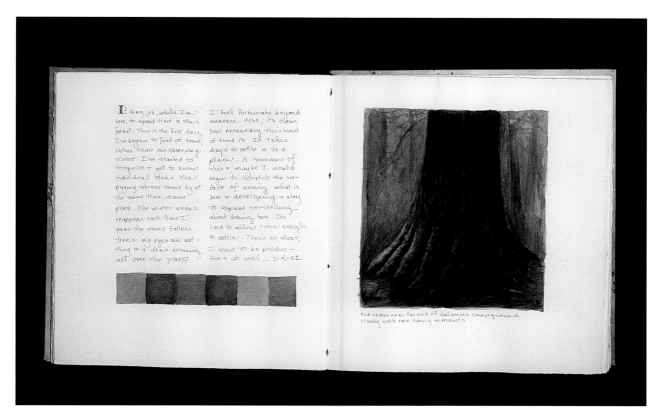

Andie Thrams

Time in the Trees (western red-cedar) | 2001–02

9 X 16½ X ⅜ INCHES (22.9 X 41.9 X 1 CM)

Arches watercolor paper, linen thread, paste paper,
gold leaf; Coptic binding; written, painted, drawn

PHOTO BY ARTIST

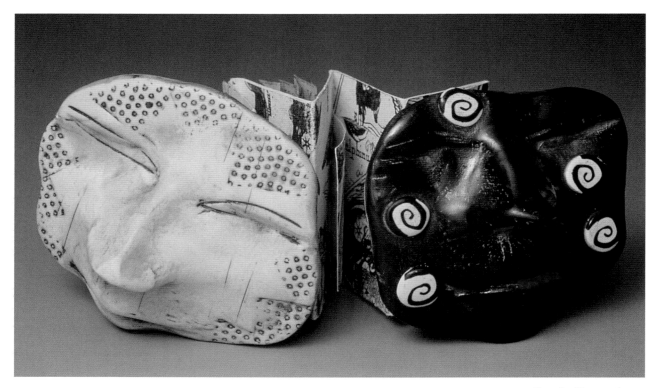

Dayle Doroshow

Mind Map | 2000

2½ X 3 X 2 INCHES (6.4 X 7.6 X 5 CM)

Polymer clay, paper; accordion binding;
carved, sculpted, millefiori

PHOTO BY DON FELTON

Evelyn Eller

Dialogue | 2005

13 X 9 X 1 INCHES (33 X 22.9 X 2.5 CM)
Handmade paper book, Lana and Oriental papers;
mixed media collage, painted, photocopy

PHOTOS BY ARTIST

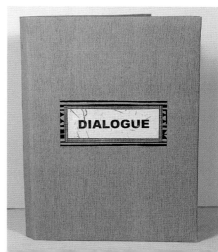

Geraldine A. Newfry

Retina | 2005

8½ X 5½ X 1½ INCHES (21.6 X 14 X 3.8 CM)

Brockway natural papers, handmade papers, polymer clay,
found objects, glass slide, medical illustration; Coptic binding

PHOTO BY LARRY SANDERS

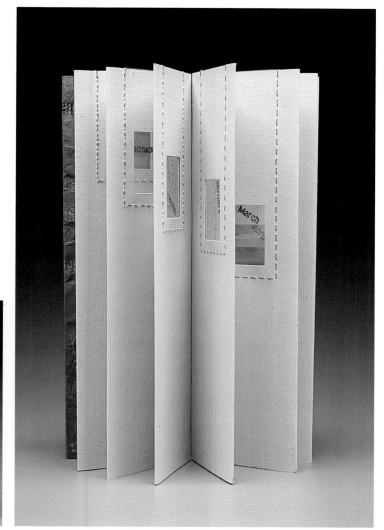

Robyn Raines

Through When | 2004

8½ X 2½ X ¾ INCHES (21.6 X 6.4 X 1.9 CM)

Art papers, Tyvek, Mylar; concertina bound; painted

PHOTOS BY ARTIST

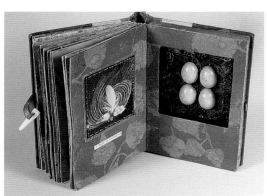

Sharon McCartney

A Constant Sound of Birds | 2004

5 X 4 X 1½ INCHES (12.7 X 10.2 X 3.8 CM)

Vintage book, ephemera and decorative papers, watercolor, acrylic, thread, feathers, found poetry, found objects, lace, wooden eggs, bone clasp; altered book, painted, drawn, photocopy transfer, gelatin printing, hand stitched

PHOTOS BY JOHN POLAK PHOTOGRAPHY
PRIVATE COLLECTION

Sharon McCartney

Collection: Nest Building | 2005

3¹/₂ X 5 X ¹/₁₀ INCHES (8.9 X 12.7 X 0.3 CM)

Elephant hide and rice paper, found poetry, ephemera, watercolor, acrylic, thread, feathers, lavender buds, stones; Coptic binding; painted, drawn, photocopy transfer, gelatin printing

PHOTO BY JOHN POLAK PHOTOGRAPHY

Carol Barton

Plant this Book | 1991

5 X 3¹⁄₄ X 2¹⁄₂ INCHES
(12.7 X 8.3 X 6.4 CM)

Found seed packets, seeds;
concertina binding; sewn

PHOTO BY ARTIST

Karen Kunc

Everything/Something | 2001

7 X 5 X 2 INCHES (17.8 X 12.7 X 5 CM)

Wood, ink, gouache; sewn binding;
screen printed, painted

PHOTOS BY LARRY FERGUSON

Miriam Timmons

Book of Vowels | 2006

2¹⁄₄ X 1¹⁄₄ X ¹⁄₂ INCHES (5.7 X 3.2 X 1.3 CM)

Nylon screen, cotton thread, embroidered letters, glass
seed beads, metal eyelets, metal chain; three ring binding

PHOTO BY ARTIST

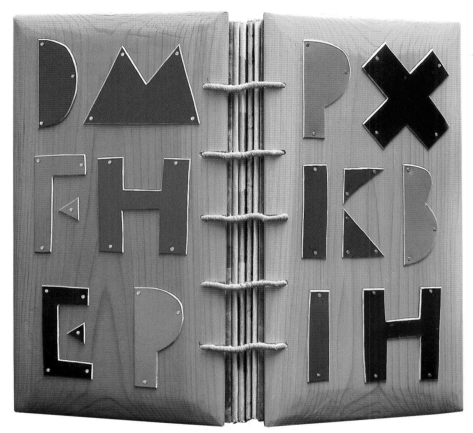

Laura Wait

Abstract Illegible #1 | 2005

11 1/8 X 6 1/2 X 1 3/4 INCHES (28.2 X 16.5 X 4.4 CM)

Cedar wood, anodized aluminum, linen thread, acrylic paint and ink, Mylar; medieval binding; painted, handwritten, stenciled

PHOTOS BY ARTIST

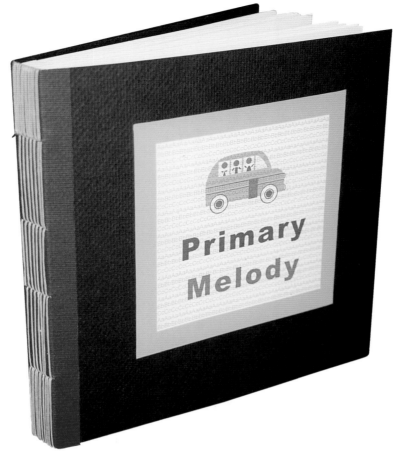

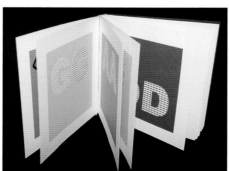

Sharon A. Sharp

Primary Melody | 2005

8 X 8 X 7/8 INCHES (20.3 X 20.3 X 2.2 CM)

Mohawk cover weight paper, Strathmore art paper, acid-free craft paper, Irish linen thread; long-stitched construction; inkjet printed, handwritten

PHOTOS BY ARTIST

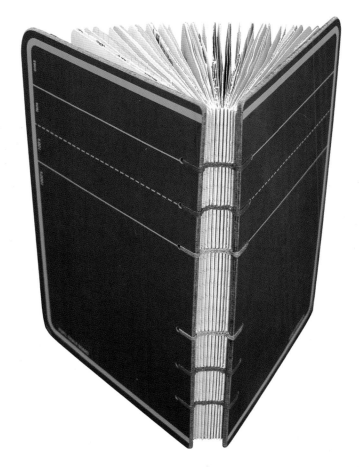

Erin Zamrzla

Chalkboard Book | 2006

9 X 6 X 1 INCHES (22.9 X 15.2 X 2.5 CM)

Chalkboard, textbook pages, antique
ruled writing paper, linen thread; Coptic
binding; individually designed pages

PHOTOS BY ARTIST

Cathy Adelman

To Everything There Is a Season | 2004

5 X 3¹/₄ X ⁵/₁₆ INCHES (12.7 X 8.3 X 0.8 CM)

Leather, paper; flyleaf, doublure; stenciled, letterpress

PHOTOS BY STEVE COHEN

Shellie Jacobson

Ha Ha Ha | 2003

11 3/4 X 6 1/4 X 3 INCHES (29.8 X 15.9 X 7.6 CM)

Rives, Mylar, Iris bookcloth; concertina
fold; drawings by artist

PHOTO BY CRAIG PHILLIPS

All except one,
And that's little Ann,
Your house is on fire
And your children alone.
For she has crept under
The frying pan.

Ladybug! Ladybug!
Fly away home.

Stephanie Dean-Moore

Ladybug, Ladybug | 2005

1 X 6 X 13 1/2 INCHES (2.5 X 15.2 X 34.3 CM)

Japanese papers, marbled papers, linen thread, brass sheet, black onyx beads; altered Coptic binding, sculpted binding; metal pierce work, riveted, inkjet printed

PHOTO BY JULIAN BEVERIDGE

Lois Morrison

Geryon's Country | 2005

5³⁄₈ X 9 X ¹⁄₂ INCHES (13.7 X 22.9 X 1.3 CM)

Arches text-wove and Fabriano Tiziano papers,
kimono material, glass buttons, grommets; tunnel
book; color copied, Gocco printed figures and sides

PHOTO BY CHARULATA DYAL

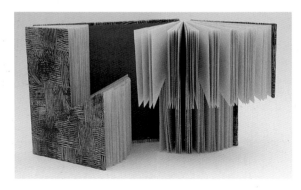

Ingrid Hein Borch

Untitled | 2006

$5^7/_8$ X $7^1/_{16}$ X $^3/_4$ INCHES (14.9 X 18 X 1.9 CM)

Book board, paste paper, dyed linen thread, acid-free text paper; Coptic binding

PHOTOS BY ALBERT J. BORCH

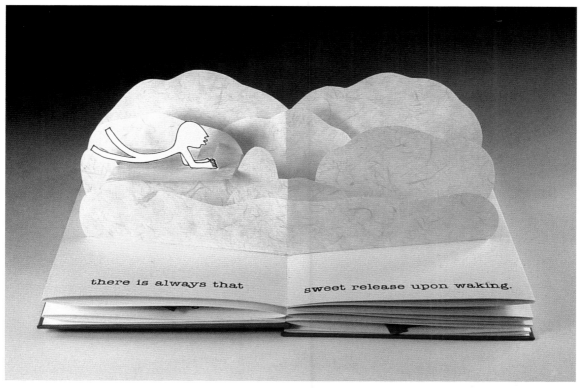

there is always that   sweet release upon waking.

Emily Martin

Sleepers, Dreamers and Screamers | 2006

9½ X 7 X 2 INCHES (24.1 X 17.8 X 5 CM)

Gampi, cotton and assorted papers;
accordion binding, pop-up; letterpress

PHOTOS BY MERYL MAREK

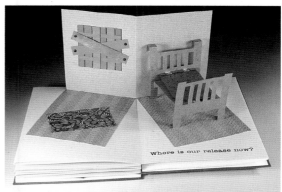

Where is our release now?

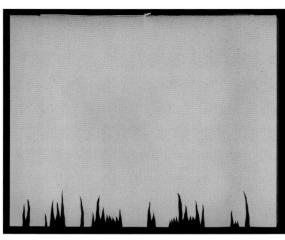

Ann Tyler
Souvenirs | 2006

7¼ X 4 X 8½ INCHES
(18.4 X 10.2 X 21.6 CM)
Crane's Lettra, photograph,
photo corners; letterpress,
inkjet printed; hand cut
PHOTOS BY ARTIST

Jody L. Williams
Condensed Creatures | 2000

1½ X 1½ X 1½ INCHES (3.8 X 3.8 X 3.8 CM)
Rives BFK paper, Chiyogami paper,
bookbinders board; accordion binding;
etched, screen printed
PHOTO BY ARTIST

Shawn Wilder Sheehy

Welcome to the Neighborwood: A Pop-Up Book of Animal Architecture | 1993

CLOSED: 8½ X 7 X 2½ INCHES (21.6 X 17.8 X 6.4 CM)

Handmade abaca/cotton paper, cotton board; letterpress, collage

PHOTO BY EDWARD DANIEL

Judith A. Hoffman

7 Extinction Events | 2006

6½ X 7 X 8 INCHES (16.5 X 17.8 X 20.3 CM)
Arches watercolor paper, plastic dinosaur, copper;
spiral binding; etched, hammered, painted, collaged
PHOTO BY ARTIST

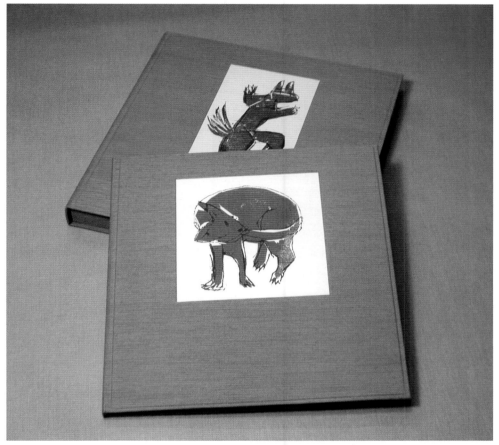

James Engelbart

Kywn, Canine, Canis | 1997

11 X 10½ X ½ INCHES (27.9 X 26.7 X 1.3 CM)

Hardbound, cloth covered; accordion structure; polymer plates, zinc relief etchings, woodblocks

PHOTOS BY ARTIST

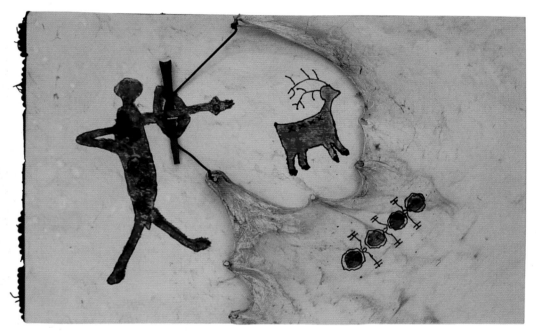

Barbara Bussolari

Untitled | 2005

6 X 9 X 1 INCHES (15.2 X 22.9 X 2.5 CM)

Nigerian goat parchment, Lotka, Strathmore drawing paper, beads, waxed linen, stick; exposed binding, woven and tied; leather dyes, computer images

PHOTOS BY NIKI KORDUS

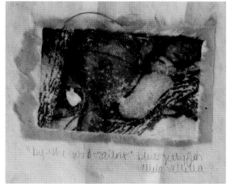

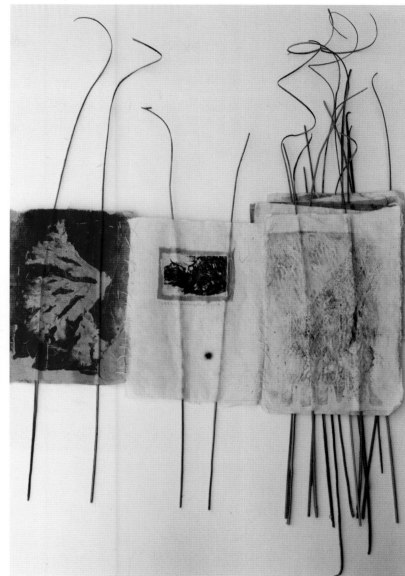

Stephanie Nace
Monterey | 2004

CLOSED: 6 X 22 INCHES (15.2 X 55.8 CM);
OPEN: 56 X 22 INCHES

Lokta paper, gelatin seaweed transfers;
hand stitching; digital prints

PHOTOS BY DENTON SMITH JR.

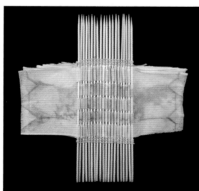

Heather Crossley

Ti (Tea) | 2006

8 X 8 X 8 INCHES (20.3 X 20.3 X 20.3 CM)
Used tea bags, sticks, beads, waxed
linen thread; piano hinge binding
PHOTOS BY ARTIST

Gail Stiffe

Red Books | 2006

9 13/16 X 11 X 7 1/16 INCHES (25 X 27.9 X 18 CM)

Overbeaten Strelitzia fiber paper; dyed, molded, watermarked, stenciled

PHOTOS BY TIM GRESHAM

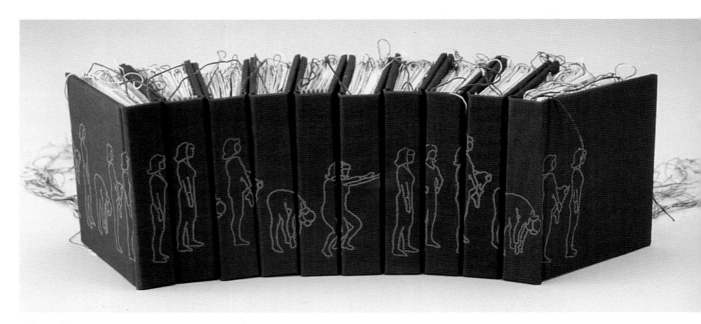

Julia Elsas

Circulatory Activities | 2004

3 1/8 X 3 1/8 X 5/8 INCHES (7.9 X 7.9 X 1.6 CM) EACH

Wallpaper, thread, cloth, board; case bound;
silkscreen; machine sewn

PHOTO BY NCMA

Susan Lenz

Some Things I'll Never Know | 2005

6½ X 13½ X 13½ INCHES (16.5 X 34.3 X 34.3 CM)

Assorted yarns and thread, assorted scraps of foreign text,
buttons; free motion machine zigzags, stitching, wrapped paper

PHOTOS BY ARTIST

Rachelle Woo Chuang
Earth & Sky/Sky & Earth | 2005

4½ X 80 X 6 INCHES (11.4 X 203.2 X 15.2 CM)

Handmade paper, denim, abaca with gelatin and mica, waxed linen thread; letterpress, dyed

PHOTOS BY DJ CHUANG

Hanne Niederhausen
Caution | 2005

OPEN: 9½ X 13 X 13 INCHES (24.1 X 33 X 33 CM);
CLOSED: 9½ X 5 X ¾ INCHES (24.1 X 12.7 X 1.9 CM)

Rives BFK, Hahnemühle photo matte, Hahnemühle Ingres, ribbons;
accordion binding; collagraph printed, inkjet printed, stenciled

PHOTOS BY ARTIST

Harry Reese

The Sea Gazer | 2003

14 5/8 X 9 1/2 X 1/2 INCHES (37.2 X 24.1 X 1.3 CM)

Monadnock Dulcet paper; flutter binding; hand-inked monotype prints from thin vinyl, digital photography and print

PHOTOS BY DOUG FARRELL

Melodie Carr

The Dot and The Line—Dual Vision Version | 2003

7 X 10 X 1³/₄ INCHES (17.8 X 25.4 X 4.4 CM)

Arch text-wove and Braille papers, Nigerian goatskin, laminated paper, silk thread, tactile graphics; letterpress, Braille and inkjet-printed text

PHOTOS BY ARTIST

Margaret Beech
Pop Up • Pop Out | 2002

2½ X 6⅛ X 2 INCHES (6.5 X 15.5 X 5 CM)
Canson Mi-Teintes and Colorplan papers, silver gouache;
accordion binding; pop-ups, cutouts; hand splashed
PHOTO BY KEN BEECH

Peter Thomas
Donna Thomas

Ukulele Series Book #4 The Ukulele Bookshelf | 1998

18 X 6 X 3 INCHES (45.7 X 15.2 X 7.6 CM)

Ukulele, leather, paper, marbled paper; accordion-fold
miniature books; gold stamped

PHOTO BY ROB THOMAS

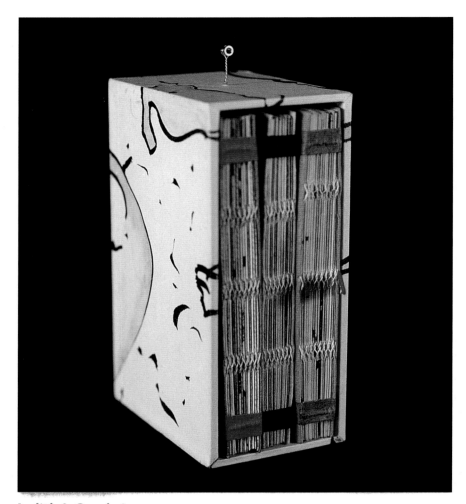

Judith I. Serebrin

U.N.* Autobiography Series, *Unified Noodle Theory | 1997

5³⁄₈ X 3³⁄₈ X 2¹⁄₄ INCHES (13.6 X 8.5 X 5.7 CM)

Text-weight watercolor paper, Japanese paper, pencil and watercolor inlays;
link and kettle-stitch exposed bindings; calligraphy, drawn

PHOTO BY ARTIST

Anita M. DeAngelis

Blank Book with Pop-Up Slip Case | 1999–2006

9¼ X 7½ X 1½ INCHES (23.5 X 19 X 3.8 CM)
Paper, linen thread, cord, ribbon; Coptic headband,
pop-up; wrapped and packed cords
PHOTO BY ARTIST

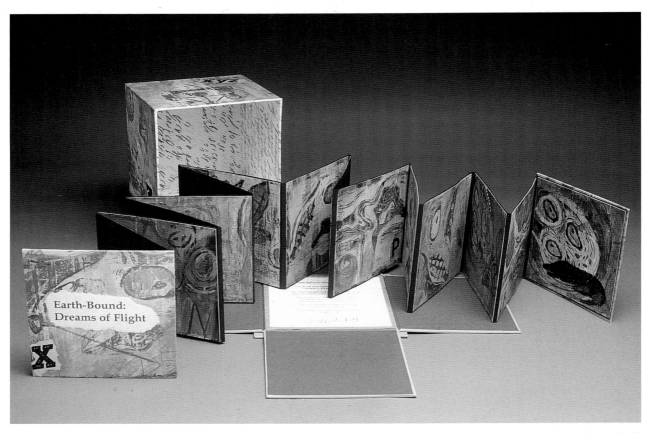

Liz Mitchell

Earth-Bound: Dreams of Flight | 2005

CLOSED: 6⅛ X 6⅛ X ½ INCHES (15.5 X 15.5 X 1.3 CM)

Arches paper; accordion binding; linocut, collage

PHOTO BY CRAIG PHILLIPS

Marilyn R. Rosenberg
Accept/Decline | 2005

6 X 3⅜ INCHES (15.2 X 8.5 CM)
Paper, gouache, ink; post binding; stenciled
PHOTO BY ARTIST

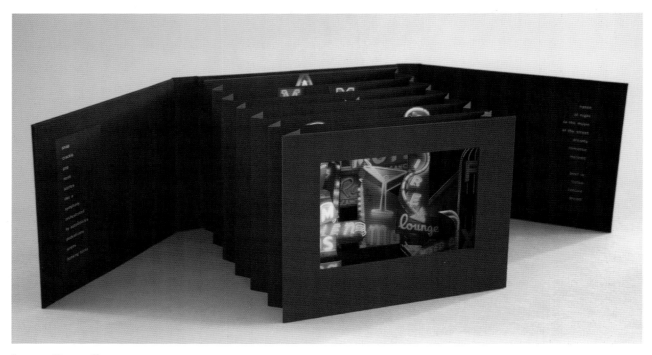

Laura Russell

Nocturne | 2005

OPEN: 8½ X 6¼ X 9 INCHES (21.6 X 15.9 X 22.9 CM)

Archival inkjet prints; tunnel book structure, wraparound cover

PHOTO BY ARTIST

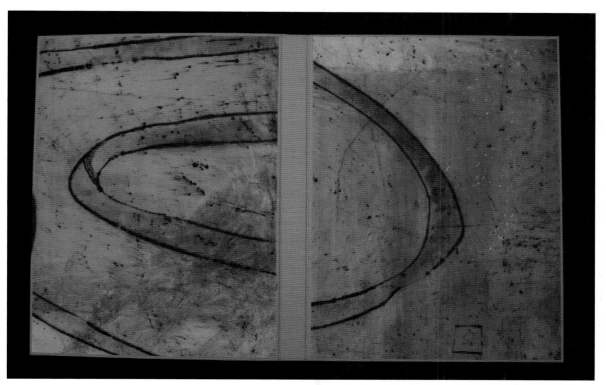

Ken Botnick

Earth Sea Sky | 2005

15 X 11 ½ X 1 INCHES (38.1 X 29.2 X 2.5 CM)

Arches paper, silk cloth over boards, gold leaf,
oil-based ink; letterpress, dry point, chine collé,
intaglio, monoprint, lettering

PHOTOS BY ARTIST

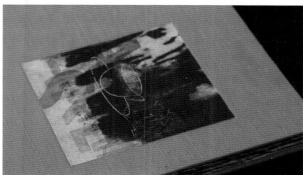

Mark Doolittle
Kathy Doolittle
Meditations | 2004

13 X 10³/₈ X 3 INCHES (33 X 26.4 X 7.6 CM)
Redwood burl, maple, African paduak, fossil
ammonite, handmade paper, waxed linen;
Coptic binding; inset fossil ammonite
PHOTO BY GEORGE POST

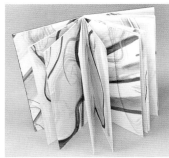

Fairley Barnes
Trails II | 2006

10 X 5¹/₂ X ¹/₂ INCHES
(25.4 X 14 X 1.3 CM)
Kozo paper, Arches cover,
string, wood, stone, silk, linen
thread, lint; link stitch binding;
painted, collaged, calligraphy
PHOTOS BY ARTIST

Mark Wangberg
David Gillespie

Colophon of Conversation | 2004

7 X 5 X ¾ INCHES (17.8 X 12.7 X 1.9 CM)
Paper, wrapping end sheets; accordion
binding; color photocopied, collaged

PHOTOS BY ARTIST

Robert Dancik

Maps, Markers and The Territory | 2005

9 X 5 X 3 INCHES (22.9 X 12.7 X 7.6 CM)

Felt, copper, Faux Bone, polymer clay, brass box hinges,
sterling silver wire, compass, paint, graphite, shoe polish,
steel; stamped, scratched, burned, embossed, die formed

PHOTOS BY DOUGLAS FOULKE

Charles Hobson

The Mappist | 2005

11 X 10 X 1¼ INCHES (27.9 X 25.4 X 3.2 CM)

Prints, transparent film, USGS maps, board;
accordion binding; digital printing

PHOTOS BY ARTIST

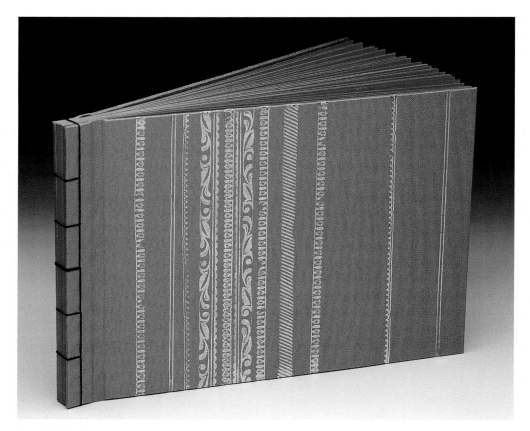

David Hodges

Orange Album | 2006

6⁷/₈ X 9¹³/₁₆ X ⁹/₁₆ INCHES (17.4 X 25 X 1.4 CM)

Canson Mi-Teintes paper, Chrome gold buckram; Japanese
stitch, five-hole procedure; hand stitched, vertical gold tooling

PHOTO BY DEREK ROSS

Valerie Ann Carrigan

Constructing Conversation | 2002

4¹/₄ X 5 X ¹/₂ INCHES (10.8 X 12.7 X 1.3 CM)

Mohawk Text paper, artist's photos and text;
accordion binding, pull-out pages; title inset;
offset lithographs, letterpress, handset type

PHOTO BY JEFF BAIRD

Laura Ann Morris

Rezidu | 2004

12 X 17½ X 3 INCHES (30.5 X 44.5 X 7.6 CM)
Wooden cigar box, blocks, roses, paint, found objects;
star fold, accordion fold, foldout tabs, tear-outs
PHOTO BY KRISTI FOSTER

Geoffrey Detrani
Raft | 2003

CLOSED: 8 X 12 INCHES (20.3 X 30.5 CM);
OPEN: 8 X 20 INCHES (20.3 X 50.8 CM)

Paper, bookbinding cloth; accordion
binding; silkscreen

PHOTOS BY ARTIST

Nisa Blackmon

Three Before Mars | 2005

3 1/2 X 4 1/2 INCHES (8.9 X 11.4 CM)

Cotton paper, vellum, glassine, waxed linen, found map, earth, grommets; double pamphlet stitching

PHOTOS BY ARTIST

Aimee Lee
Sari Book | 2003

7½ X 5 X 1 INCHES (19 X 12.7 X 2.5 CM)

Sari cloth, thread, flax seeds, tea bags;
pen on cloth, hand sewn

PHOTOS BY EDWARD DANIEL

Dennis Yuen

Oversquared Faux Suede | 2006

5 X 5 1/4 X 13/16 INCHES (12.7 X 13.3 X 2.1 CM)

Laval bookcloth, decorative paper, Davey board, linen threads; long stitch binding

PHOTOS BY ARTIST

Chris Bivins

Untitled | 2005

6 X 12 INCHES (15.2 X 30.5 CM)
Paper, leather, found objects, basic codex
PHOTO BY ARTIST

Sylvia Ramos Alotta

The Diary of Victor Frankenstein | 2005

13 X 10 X 25 INCHES (33 X 25.4 X 63.5 CM)
Mixed media, leather, cloth; fine design binding

PHOTOS BY ARTIST

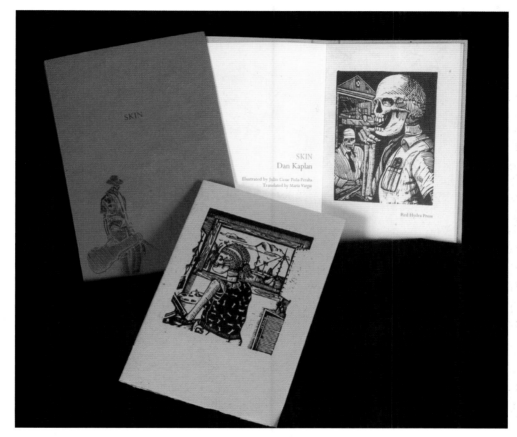

Steve Miller

Skin *by Dan Kaplan, translated by Maria Vargas* | 2005

8 X 5 X ¹/₈ INCHES (20.3 X 12.7 X 0.3 CM)
Nideggen moldmade text paper, Khadi handmade paper;
letterpress, linocuts, photopolymer plates

PHOTO BY ARTIST
LINOCUTS BY JULIO CESAR PEÑA PERALTA, HAVANA, CUBA

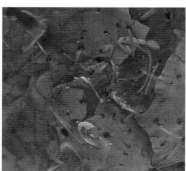

Jessie Lehson

Seasons Book | 2001

5 X 6 X 3 INCHES (12.7 X 15.2 X 7.6 CM)

Rives BFK paper, leaves, thread, paint, stick, twine, beeswax; modified stab binding; hand sewn

PHOTOS BY ARTIST

Diane Cassidy

A Plethora of Petroglyphs | 2005

10 X 7 X 1 INCHES (25.4 X 17.8 X 2.5 CM)

Davey board, Canson Mi-Teintes pastel paper, original photos;
accordion binding; carved, torn, stamped, reverse printed

PHOTOS BY ARTIST

Debra Meyer

Untitled | 2004

7 X 4½ X 1³/₈ INCHES (17.8 X 11.4 X 3.5 CM)

Hardwood, linen thread, handmade paper,
Arches text wove; Coptic stitch

PHOTO BY ARTIST

Kathryn Rodenbach

Afghan Post Butterflies | 2006

4³⁄₈ X 20 X ³⁄₈ INCHES (11 X 50.8 X 0.9 CM)

Japanese paper, matte board, pastel paper, mulberry paper, metal embellishment, Afghan stamps, ribbon; accordion binding; collaged

PHOTOS BY CARRIE CLAYCOMB

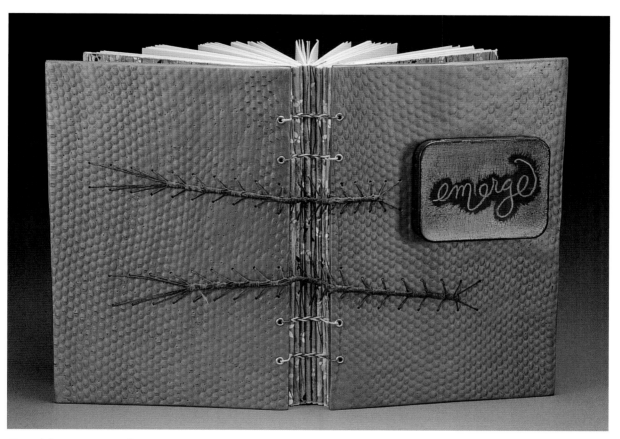

Geraldine A. Newfry

Emerge: Two Options | 2004

8½ X 5½ X 1½ INCHES (21.6 X 14 X 3.8 CM)

Brockway natural papers, Japanese paper, polymer clay, metal tin, colored pencil, resin, butterfly, waxed linen; Coptic binding, caterpillar stitch

PHOTO BY GUY NICOL

Linda L. Broadfoot

INSECTA | 2005

Mold-made and handmade papers, silk, organza, linen thread, ragboard, maple, poplar, brass hardware; long stitch sewn signatures, half-bound portfolio binding; letterpress, inkjet printed, embossed

PHOTOS BY DARYL BUNN

Constance K. Wozny

In the Time of the Butterflies | 2006

8³/₄ X 5⁷/₈ X 1¹/₄ INCHES (22.2 X 14.9 X 3.2 CM)

Handmade marble paper, goat leather, black foil letters; case binding; colored edges, relief

PHOTO BY ARTIST

Dorothy A. Yule

Doyle the Loyal Royal | 2003

BOOK: 2³/₄ X 2¹³/₁₆ X 1³/₈ INCHES (7 X 7.3 X 3.4 CM);
BOX: 3⁷/₈ X 3⁷/₈ X 2¹/₂ INCHES (9.8 X 9.8 X 6.4 CM)

Mohawk Superfine, museum boards, tulle, cellophane, clear plastic
sheeting; tunnel book, rotating wheel, pulley tabs; laser printed

PHOTO BY ARTIST

Dorothy A. Yule

Memories of Science | 1996–2007

BOOK: 2³/₄ X 2¹³/₁₆ X 1³/₈ INCHES (7 X 7.2 X 3.5 CM)

Mohawk Superfine, Sekishu, wasp nest paper;
concertina, French fold text, pop-up illustration,
folded covers; letterpress, laser printed

PHOTOS BY ARTIST

Peter Thomas
Donna Thomas

Ukulele Series Book #9, The Letterpress Ukulele | 2002

18 X 6 X 3 INCHES (45.7 X 15.2 X 7.6 CM)
Ukulele, brass, handmade paper, metal bands;
sewn, letterpress, woodcut, linoleum cut

PHOTO BY ROB THOMAS

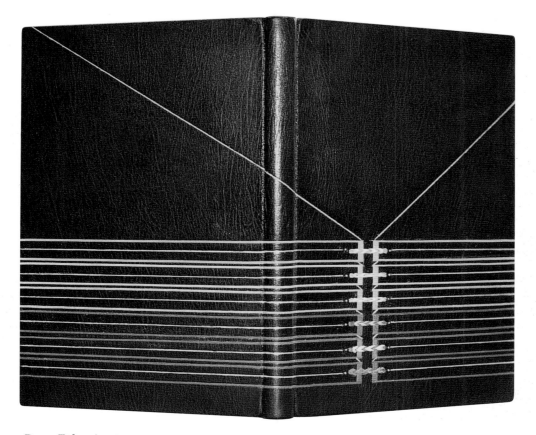

Don Etherington

Recollections *by Bernard Middleton* | 1996

10¹/₈ X 6⁵/₈ X ³/₄ INCHES (25.7 X 16.8 X 1.9 CM)

Goatskin and goatskin onlays, doublures, flyleaves, Japanese paper;
link-stitch binding; gold tooling, braided thong bands

PHOTO BY ARTIST

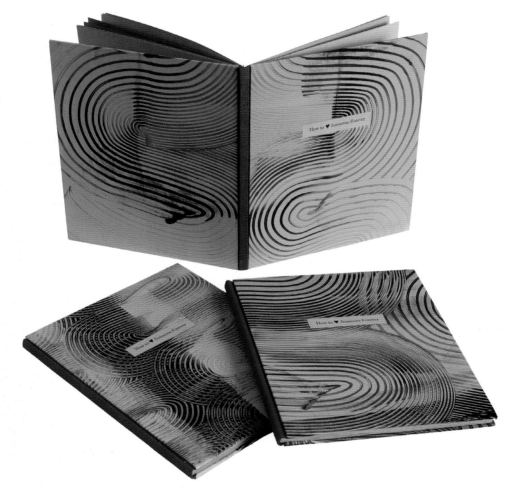

Ellen Knudson

How to Love Someone Forever | 2004

6 X 8 INCHES (15.2 X 20.3 CM)

Hahnemühle mold-made Bugra papers, handmade paste-paper covers; double pamphlet sewn in German-lapped style case binding; letterpress, handset metal types, photopolymer plates

PHOTOS BY MEGAN BEAN

Linda K. Johnson

The Nightingale and the Rose | 2005

14½ X 11 X ½ INCHES (36.8 X 27.9 X 1.3 CM)

Rives heavyweight, Fabriano Tiziano papers, fabric hard covers, brocade fabric slipcase; sewn binding; letterpress printed, watercolor pochoir illustration

PHOTOS BY ARTIST

Alexis Adams
1000 Leaves for My Love | 2005

3 X 3 X 3 INCHES (7.6 X 7.6 X 7.6 CM)
Moriki, silk cording; etched
PHOTOS BY ARTIST

Joanne Kluba
At Home on Earth | 2004

4 X 5 X 4½ INCHES (10.2 X 12.7 X 11.4 CM)
Vellum, Cave paper, Japanese silk bookcloth,
reclaimed textbooks, linen thread; Coptic
binding; watercolor
PHOTO BY ARTIST

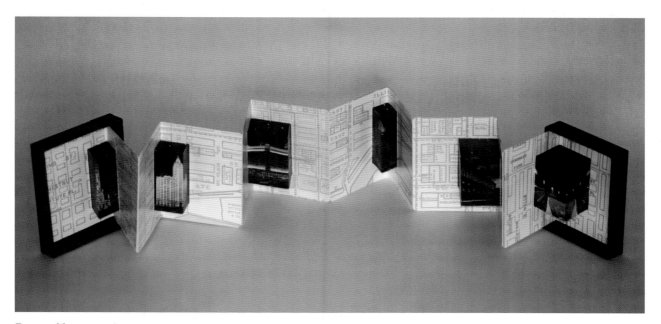

Betsy Kruger

Chicago | 2006

5 5/8 X 56 X 1/2 INCHES (14.3 X 142.2 X 1.3 CM)

Somerset paper, paste papers, binders board, bookcloth, vintage map, postcards; accordion format bound into box; inkjet printed

PHOTO BY GAVIN SUNTOP

Mary Ellen Long

Peace | 2005

CLOSED: 7½ X 6½ X ¾ INCHES (19 X 16.5 X 1.9 CM);
OPEN: 7½ X 14½ X ¾ INCHES (19 X 36.8 X 1.9 CM)

Nepal mango and Lokta papers, Davey board,
waxed linen thread; Coptic binding; sanded, inked

PHOTOS BY ARTIST

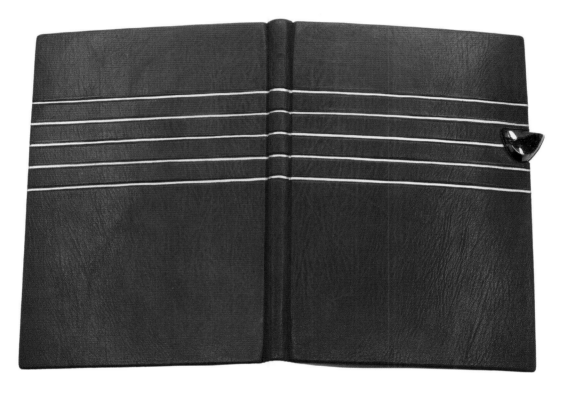

David John Lawrence

The Song of Songs Which Is Solomon's | 2004

9 5/8 X 6 5/8 X 5/8 INCHES (24. 5 X 16.8 X 1.6 CM)

Goatskin, marbled paper by Catherine Levine, calfskin, druzy hematite, sterling silver, graphite, hand embroidered; fine binding; stone setting by Michelle Freeman

PHOTO BY BOBBY BADGER

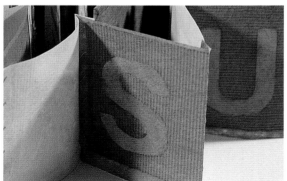

Maria G. Pisano

XYZ | 2001

CLOSED: 2½ X 2¾ X ½ INCHES (6.5 X 7.2 X 1.2 CM)

Handmade paper, abaca fiber; watermark letter design;
accordion binding

PHOTOS BY ARTIST

Emily Martin

Mutually Exclusive | 2002

6 ¼ X 4 ¼ X 1 ¼ INCHES (15.9 X 10.8 X 3.2 CM)

Magic wallets; Japanese box wrapper; letterpress;
bone clasps by Rosa Guimaraes.

PHOTOS BY MERYL MAREK

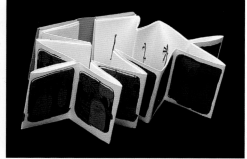

Ryan Cecil Smith
The Disagreeable Ghost | 2006

1³⁄₄ X 1¹⁄₂ X ⁵⁄₈ INCHES (4.4 X 3.8 X 1.6 CM)

Paper, chipboard label; accordion folded;
screen printed, bagged, stapled

PHOTOS BY ABBY UHTEG

Cathryn Miller
no skateboarding | 2005

CLOSED: 3 X 3 X 3 INCHES (7.6 X 7.6 X 7.6 CM);
OPEN: 10 X 24¹⁄₂ INCHES (25.4 X 62.2 CM)

Acid-free cardstock, paper; bustrophedon
variation; digital photography, paper
engineering, giclée print

PHOTOS BY DAVID G. MILLER

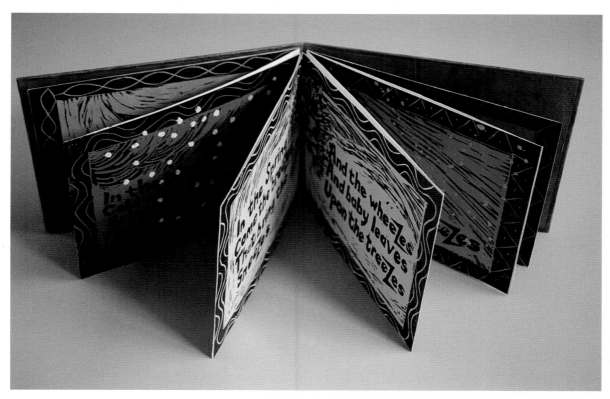

Frances Watson

Breezes | 2005

6³/₄ X 8¹/₂ INCHES (17.2 X 21.6 CM)

Book board, Rives Heavy paper, paint, ink; accordion
binding; painted, stenciled, linocut, hand printed, hinged

PHOTO BY ARTIST

Susan Collard

The Winter Palace | 2006

4½ X 3½ X 2½ INCHES (11.4 X 8.9 X 6.4 CM)

Walnut, birch aircraft plywood, glass, steel, basswood, Tyvek, reclaimed tongue-and-groove fir covers, brass, magnetic closures; piano-hinged structure, two perfect-bound miniature books; mixed media collage

PHOTOS BY ARTIST

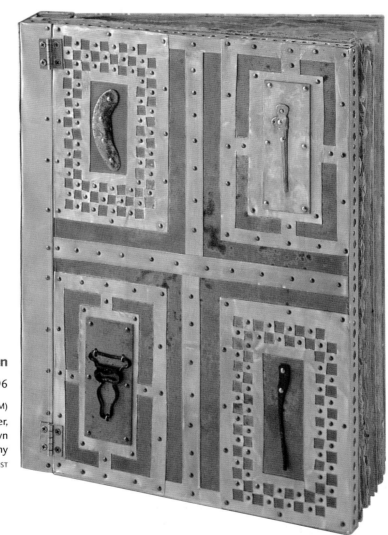

Peter Madden

Ireland Journal | 1996

11 X 8½ X 2 INCHES (27.9 X 21.6 X 5 CM)

Copper, found metal, wood, paper, wax; modified Japanese side-sewn binding; lithography

PHOTO BY ARTIST

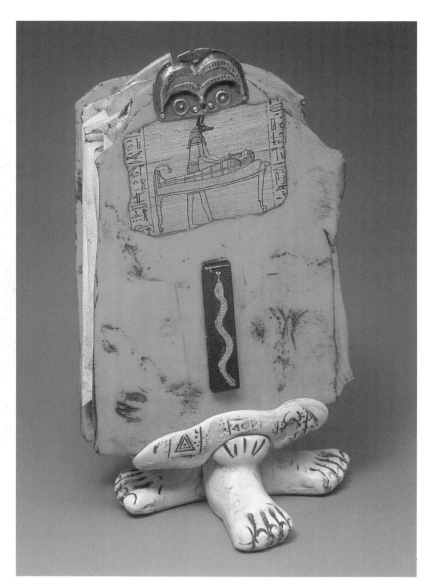

Dayle Doroshow
Egyptian Spell Book | 2004

6 X 3 X 1½ INCHES (15.2 X 7. 6 X 3.8 CM)
Polymer clay, metallic powders; accordion
binding; sculpted, carved, painted
PHOTO BY DON FELTON

Claudia Lee
Untitled | 2005

4 X 3 X ½ INCHES (10.2 X 7.6 X 1.3 CM)

Handmade and commercial papers, natural dyes,
waxed linen; Coptic binding; wax resist, stitched

PHOTO BY JOHN LUCAS

Marie C. Oedel

4 Tacketed Bindings | 2004

6³/₈ X 4⁵/₁₆ X 1³/₁₆ INCHES (16.2 X 11 X 3 CM)
Airplane linen, Mohawk vellum, leather;
tacket binding; hand dyed

PHOTO BY DEAN POWELL

Emily Gold

Dormancy | 2006

11 ½ X 11 ½ X 2 ½ INCHES
(29.2 X 29.2 X 6.4 CM)

Matte board, Arches
watercolor paper, mixed
media; altered
accordion fold

PHOTOS BY STEVEN TRUBITT

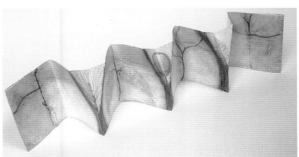

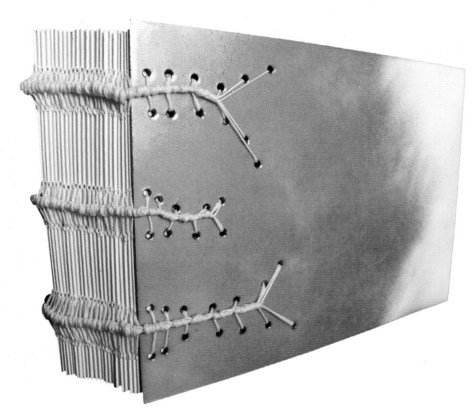

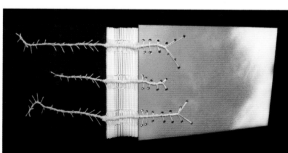

E. Bond

Rising | 2006

7 X 5 X 1¼ INCHES (17.8 X 12.7 X 3.2 CM)

Copper plate, linen thread; caterpillar
binding; drilled, fired, sewn

PHOTOS BY SIOBHAN EDMONDS

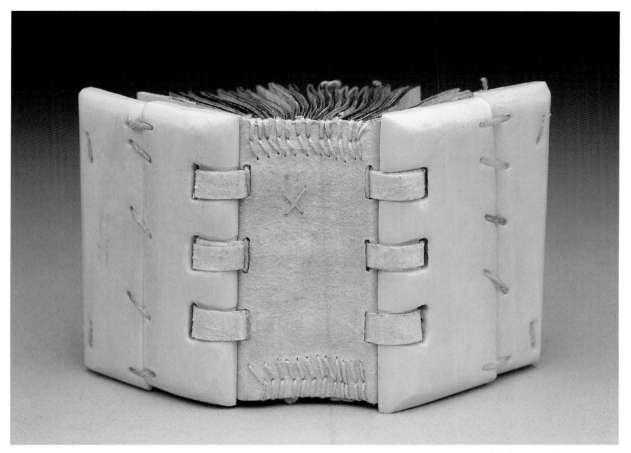

Shanna Leino

Dear Ben Brown Eyes | 2005

2½ X 1¾ X 1½ INCHES (6.4 X 4.4 X 3.8 CM)

Elk bone, linen thread, flax paper, sinew, parchment, graphite

PHOTOS BY WALKER MONTGOMERY

Laura Russell

Nippon | 2004

OPEN: 2³/₄ X 3 X 59 INCHES (7 X 7.6 X 149.9 CM)

Arches paper, black goatskin, acrylic paint; collage, painted

PHOTOS BY ARTIST

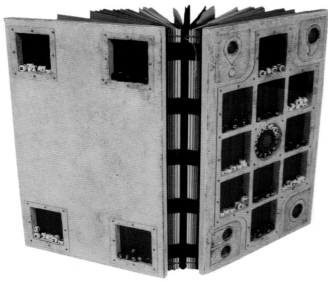

Dolph Smith

Reading-Writing: A Tennarkippi Journal or Everything You Want in a Good Book | 2005

93/4 X 61/2 X 2 INCHES (24.7 X 16.5 X 5 CM)

Wood, milk paint, polycarbonate, acrylic, bookcloth, beads, mixed papers; multi-section binding on tapes; stamped

PHOTO BY ARTIST

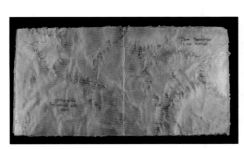

Jennifer Hines

Skin | 2004

CLOSED: 8 X 8 INCHES (20.3 X 20.3 CM)

Rice paper, ink, thread, beeswax; Coptic binding; tea-dyed paper, stitched

PHOTOS BY ARTIST

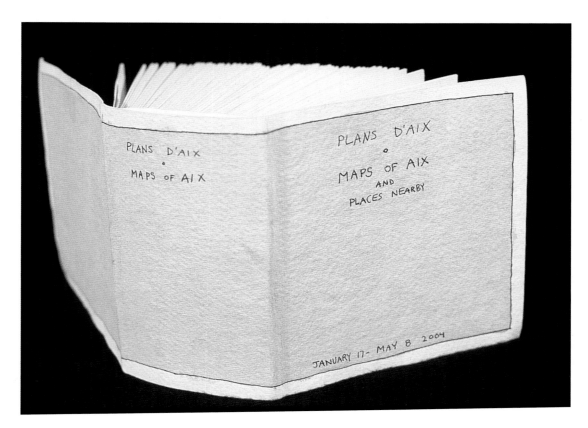

Val Lucas

Plans d'Aix | 2005

5 X 5 X 3 INCHES (12.7 X 12.7 X 7.6 CM)
Watercolor and pen on Fabriano
cold press; accordion binding, sewn
PHOTO BY ARTIST

James Cohen

People | 2001

6 X 6 X ½ INCHES (15.2 X 15.2 X 1.3 CM)

Coptic binding; letterpress

PHOTO BY SALLY ANN PHOTOGRAPHY

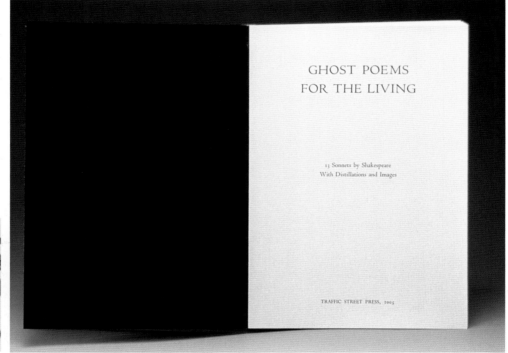

GHOST POEMS
FOR THE LIVING

13 Sonnets by Shakespeare
With Distillations and Images

TRAFFIC STREET PRESS, 2005

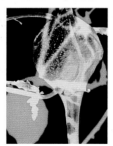

Paulette Myers-Rich

Ghost Poems for the Living: 13 Sonnets by Shakespeare with Distillations | 2005

8 X 12 X 1½ INCHES (20.3 X 30.5 X 3.8 CM)

Photo rag paper, handmade flax paper, boards, linen; hand bound; letterpress, slipcase in linen, digital inkjet printed

PHOTOS BY ARTIST

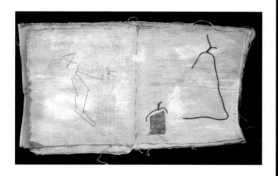

Beata Wehr

Zeszyt O Czasie (On Time) | 2006

10 X 8½ X ¾ INCHES (25.4 X 21.6 X 1.9 CM)

Linen, gesso, metal objects, linen thread, ink

PHOTOS BY ARTIST

Debra Fink Bachelder

Head Case | 2004

CLOSED: 7 X 7 X 3 INCHES (17.8 X 17.8 X 7.6 CM);
OPEN: 7 X 14 X 7½ INCHES (17.8 X 35.6 X 19 CM)

Recycled CDs, reclaimed medical display, screw post,
safety pins, padded cover; rubber stamped, handwritten

PHOTOS BY ARTIST

Benjamin D. Rinehart

sissy | 2004

4½ X 6½ X ¼ INCHES (11.4 X 16.5 X 0.6 CM)

Archival inkjet paper, binders board, bookcloth; perfect
bound with flat-backed case; digital printed images

PHOTOS BY ARTIST

Diane Talbot

Time to Play | 2003

5 X 8 X ½ INCHES (12.7 X 20.3 X 1.3 CM)

Paper, clip art, found items; paper hinged

PHOTOS BY ARTIST

Cristina Pinton

Diary, Evidence, Language, Record—San Nicolo Dei Mendicoli, Venezia | 2006

5³/₄ X 5³/₄ X ³/₄ INCHES (15 X 15 X 2 CM)

Chinese paper, paper, board, clamshell box, loose pages, clear plastic sheeting; copy transfer, dry point, relief work

PHOTO BY ARTIST

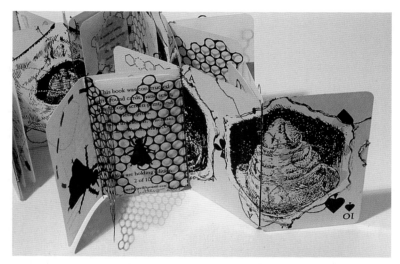

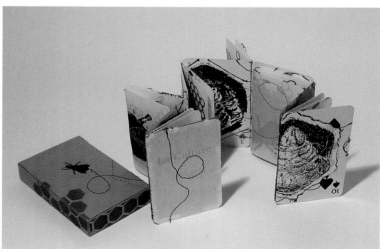

Carey Watters

Bee Culture | 2004

4 X 2½ X ⅝ INCHES (10.2 X 6.4 X 1.6 CM)

Found cards, transparent paper, plastic ribbon; hand stitched, silkscreen, photocopy, letterpress

PHOTOS BY ARTIST

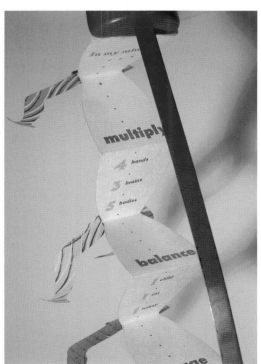

Carey Watters

Multiply | 2004

5 X 3 X ½ INCHES (12.7 X 7.6 X 1.3 CM)

Found objects; accordion binding; silkscreened, letterpress

PHOTOS BY ARTIST

Cody Calhoun

This I Know as of 2006 | 2006

22 X 4½ X 3 INCHES (55.9 X 11.4 X 7.6 CM)

Vintage German doll head, historic box, paste paper, wood, waxed linen, mica, polymer clay, shrink plastic, buttons, beads, dominoes, ribbon; various Origami and accordion folds; flag and palm-leaf book structure in miniature

PHOTO BY ARTIST

Thery McKinney

Pips and Proverbs | 2003

2 X 9 INCHES (5.1 X 22.9 CM)

L'Amatruda/Amalfi and Arches paper, ribbon; accordion binding on dominoes; computer printed, watercolor, calligraphy

PHOTO BY ARTIST

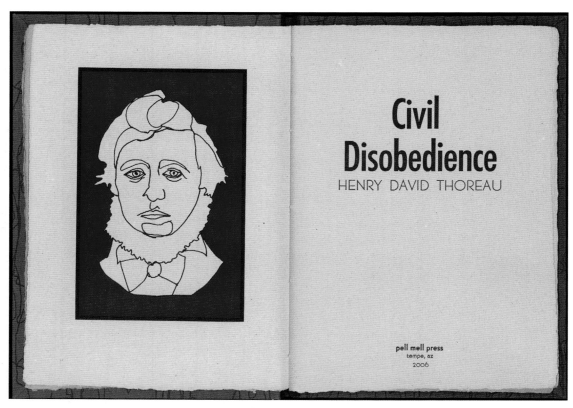

Ashlee Weitlauf

Civil Disobedience | 2006

6 X 9 INCHES (15.2 X 22.9 CM)

Handmade paper; letterpress, pamphlet, photopolymer plates, handset type

PHOTOS BY ARTIST

Ellen Knudson

How Swimming Saved My Life | 2005

6⅝ X 9½ INCHES (16.8 X 24.1 CM)

Somerset book heavyweight paper, Indian Khadi paper; pamphlet sewn;
letterpress, handset metal types, gelatin plate monoprint

PHOTO BY MEGAN BEAN

Steve Miller

Design/Diseño *by Billy Collins, translated by Maria Vargas*

8⅝ X 5⅝ X ⅜ INCHES (21.9 X 14.3 X 1 CM)
Cuban recycled handmade paper, Bugra text papers,
paste paper; multiple-signature sewn binding; letterpress,
linocuts, photopolymer plates

PHOTO BY ARTIST
LINOCUTS BY CARLOS AYRESS MORENO
BOOKBINDING DESIGN BY ANNA EMBREE

Peter Thomas
Donna Thomas

Y2K3MS: Ukulele Series Book #2, Ukulele Accordion | 1996

18 X 6 X 3 INCHES (45.7 X 15.2 X 7.6 CM)
Ukulele, leather, leather onlay, sound hole, handmade paper;
accordion binding; handwritten, illustrated

PHOTO BY ROB THOMAS

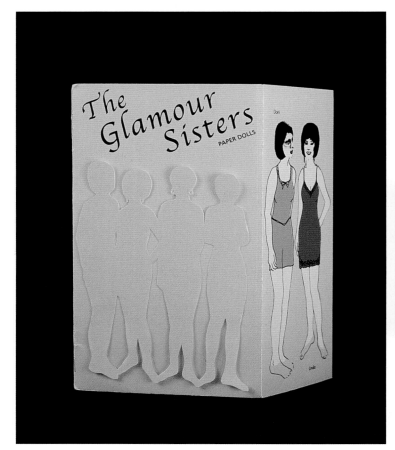

Marcia Weisbrot

The Glamour Sisters Paper Dolls | 2003

7 X 10½ INCHES (17.8 X 26.7 CM)

Original watercolor and ink drawings;
laser copied, screen-printed cover

PHOTOS BY ARTIST

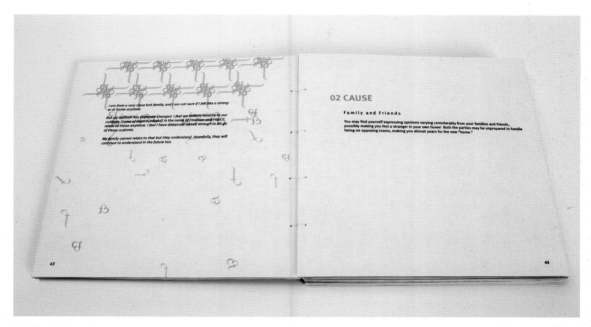

Malini Gupta

From Familiar to Unfamiliar | 2005

1 ½ X 8 X 8 INCHES (3.8 X 20.3 X 20.3 CM)

Wausau white paper; French folded, Coptic single-sheet
binding; inkjet printed; custom-made clamshell box

PHOTO BY ARTIST AND ELLIOT OLSON

QUICK STITCHES

BY ANNA MARIE OTTAVIANO

CROSS STITCH   FLY STITCH

Anna Marie Ottaviano
Quick Stitches | 2004

8 X 10 X ½ INCHES (20.3 X 25.4 X 1.3 CM)
Yupo, Fabriano Rosaspina, cotton thread; accordion binding, blanket stitched; hand sewn, forged, lithography, intaglio
PHOTOS BY ARTIST

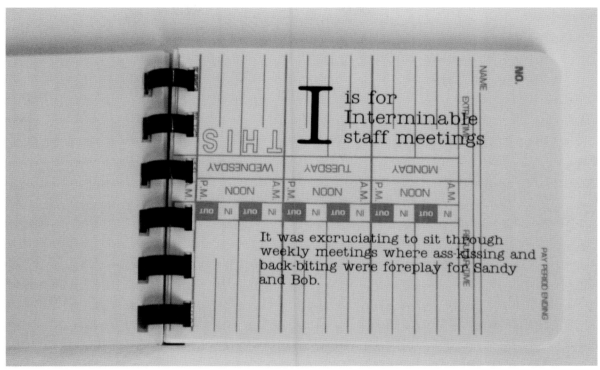

Roberta Lavadour

Office Politics Alphabet: A Story in 26 Parts | 2004

3 ½ X 5 ¼ X ½ INCHES (8.9 X 13.3 X 1.3 CM)

File dividers, time cards; comb binding;
laser and letterpress printed

PHOTOS BY ARTIST

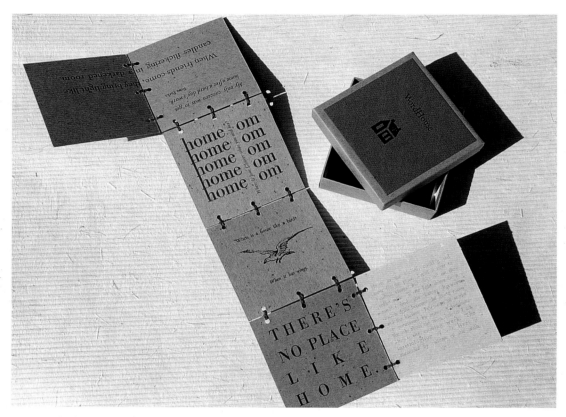

Bonnie Thompson Norman

WordHouse | 1999

6 1/2 X 3 1/4 X 3 1/4 INCHES (16.5 X 8.3 X 8.3 CM)

Chipboard, colored paper, kraft-paper box, waxed linen thread, ink; edge binding; sewn, letterpress, colophon, handset types, rubber stamped

PHOTO BY ARTIST

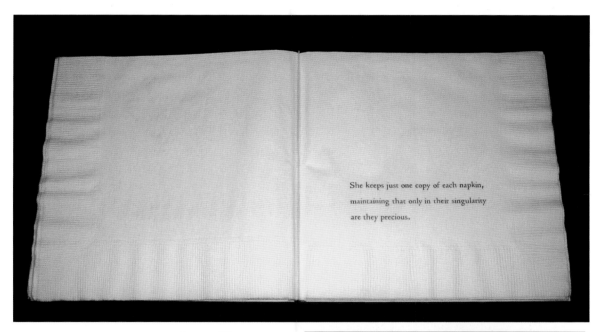

She keeps just one copy of each napkin, maintaining that only in their singularity are they precious.

Anne Thompson

My Mother's Napkins | 2004

7 X 7 X ¾ INCHES (17.8 X 17.8 X 1.9 CM)

Paper napkins, bookcloth over board, Tosa Hanga;
modified concertina; letterpress-printed metal type,
photopolymer plates

PHOTOS BY ARTIST

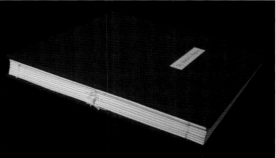

Maria Rogal

7 Minutes 3 Seconds: Mérida en Domingo | 2005

3³/₄ X 3³/₄ X 2 INCHES (9.5 X 9.5 X 5 CM)

Accordion binding; inkjet printed

PHOTOS BY ARTIST

Jan Owen

Dies Irae | 2005

46 X 15½ INCHES (116.8 X 39.4 CM)

Paper, acrylic, and Sumi ink, Tyvek;
accordion binding; painted, woven

PHOTOS COURTESY OF SEWANEE, THE UNIVERSITY OF THE SOUTH

Gabrielle Fox

With Jazz *by Bobbie Ann Mason* | 2006

8½ X 6 X ⁹/₁₆ INCHES (21.5 X 15 X 1.5 CM)

Goatskin, onlays and doublures, silk thread, gold leaf; tooled

PHOTO BY ALICE M. CORNELL

Laura Wait

The Other Goddess in the Garden | 2005

10½ X 5¾ X ¾ INCHES (26.7 X 14.6 X 1.9 CM)

Arches cover paper, Mylar, leather, wood, parchment, acrylic paint, artist's pens; modified simple binding, exposed sewing on concertina; painted, handwritten

PHOTOS BY ARTIST

Janet Lorch

Nature's Brush | 2006

10 X 7¼ X ¾ INCHES (25.4 X 18.4 X 1.9 CM)

Bookcloth, leaves, photo paper;
exposed binding; digital printing

PHOTO BY ARTIST

Bridget A. Elmer

The Reader | 2006

4 X 4 X ⅛ INCHES (10.2 X 10.2 X 0.3 CM)

Japanese kozo, handmade paper, waxed linen thread, organdy cover; double pamphlet-stitch binding; collograph, chine-collé, letterpress, hand-cut petals

PHOTO BY STEVE MANN

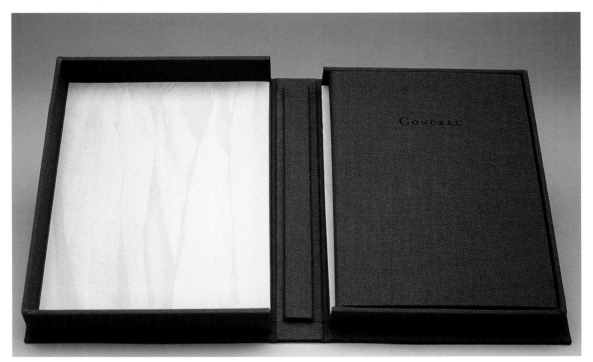

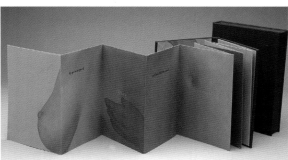

Cynthia Thompson

Conceal | 2006

6 X 44 X ½ INCHES (15.2 X 110 X 1.3 CM)

Handmade pigmented cotton paper;
French fold accordion binding; letterpress,
digital imagery, clamshell box

PHOTOS BY ARTIST

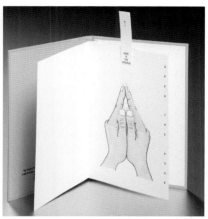

Stephanie Wolff

Ten Fingers Play | 2004

6³/₁₆ X 4³/₁₆ X ⁵/₁₆ INCHES (15.7 X 10.7 X 0.8 CM)

Paper, bookcloth, binders board; concertina codex;
color and laser copy

PHOTOS BY JOHN SHERMAN

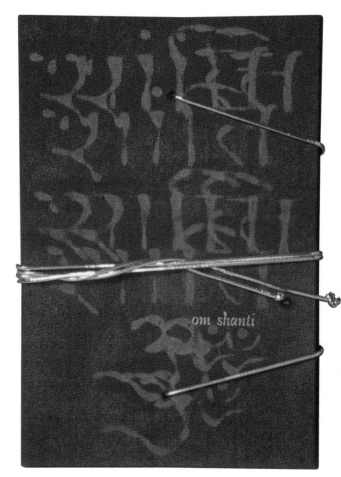

Tara O'Brien
Om Shanti | 2005

7½ X 18 X 4 INCHES (19 X 45.7 X 10.2 CM)
Hahnemühle Bugra paper; flag book;
pressure print, letterpress
PHOTOS BY ARTIST

Mira Coviensky
Cribbage Time | 2004

13 X 3 X 2½ INCHES (33 X 7.6 X 6.4 CM)

Plastic cribbage board, pegs, aluminum leaf, Pantypress, cork, and kozuke papers, found object, family photographs; accordion binding; laser printed, collage, handwritten

PHOTOS BY PIITZ-NAZAR

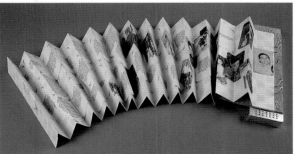

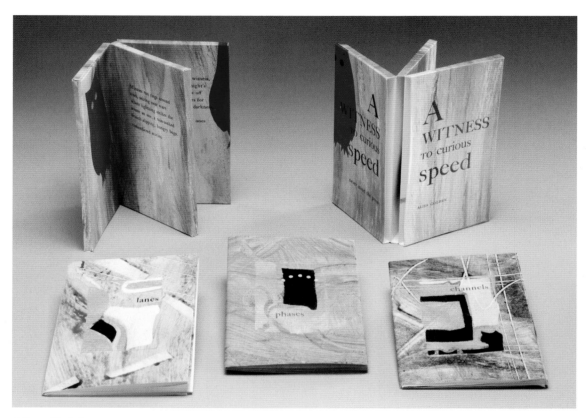

Alisa Golden

A Witness to Curious Speed | 2005

5½ X 3¾ INCHES (14 X 9.5 CM)

Paper, paste paper; triple slipcase;
letterpress, painted, stenciled

PHOTO BY SIBILA SAVAGE

Susan Weinz

The Incomplete Book of Pesto (with Slipcase) | 2003

4½ X 6¼ X ½ INCHES (11.4 X 15.9 X 1.3 CM)

Various papers, tabbed recipe cards; accordion
with flags and fold-out pages; collage, photocopied,
rubber stamped, inkjet printed

PHOTO BY PEGGY MCKENNA

I got a picture postcard with some poetry sticks on it. They looked like twigs wrapped in paper, but I was told they were more like walking sticks with poetry painted on them, all in French. Word sticks to help you walk through life.

Alisa Golden

Wrapped in Their Offspring | 2004

BOOK: 10¹/₄ X 3¹/₄ INCHES (26 X 8.3 CM)

Paper, museum board, glassine, camphor sticks, acrylic inks, gesso; accordion binding; letterpress, linocut

PHOTO BY SIBILA SAVAGE

Susan T. Viguers

Portrait of a Daughter: Ruth's Room | 2002

CLOSED: 5³/₄ X 5¹/₂ X ⁵/₈ INCHES (14.6 X 14 X 1.6 CM)

Rives BFK, linen thread, cotton cloth; case binding, caterpillar stitching; handset metal type, letterpress, monoprints

PHOTO BY KAREN MAUCH

Shanna Leino

Untitled | 2005

3½ X 2¼ X ¾ INCHES (8.9 X 5.7 X 1.9 CM)

Cedar, milk paint, linen thread, silk, and cotton cloth; Coptic binding; stitched, monoprint

PHOTOS BY NANCY BELLUSCIO

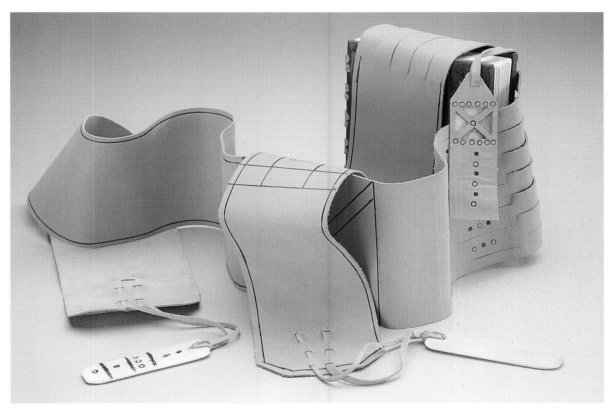

Marie C. Oedel

Leather Crossbook | 2002

5 1/4 X 4 3/4 X 1 1/2 INCHES (13.5 X 12 X 4 CM)

Mohawk vellum, linen thread, leather, wood;
multi-quire Coptic codex; sewn, carbon tooled

PHOTOS BY DEAN POWELL

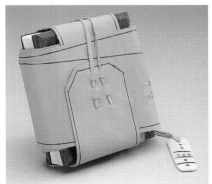

Robbin Ami Silverberg

Spun Into Gold: First 100 Words | 2002

7 X 5¼ X 1½ INCHES (17.8 X 13.3 X 3.8 CM)
Dobbin Mill kozo papers; case binding; archival
inkjet printed, hand-cut and spun paper
PHOTO BY GREGG ST-ANGER

Deena Schnitman
Untitled | 2003

BOOKS: 6³/₄ X 5 X 1¹/₂ INCHES (17.2 X 12.7 X 3.8 CM);
CASE: 7 X 4 X 5¹/₄ INCHES (17.8 X 10.2 X 13.3 CM)

Handmade paste paper, acid-free textblock,
bookcloth, waxed linen, seed beads;
long-stitch binding

PHOTO BY JEFF BAIRD

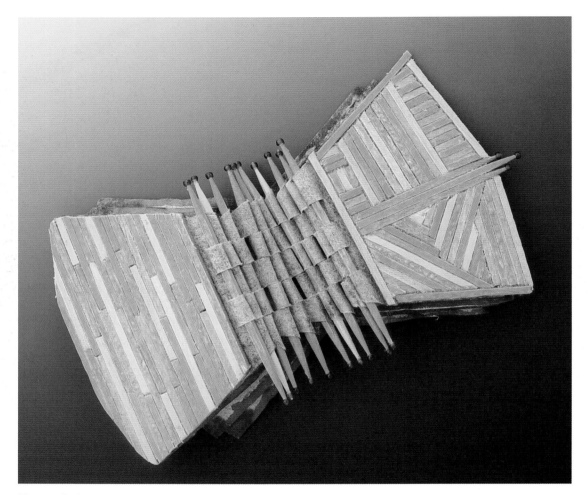

Karen J. Lauseng

Untitled | 2006

4½ X 3 X 5 INCHES (11.4 X 7.6 X 12.7 CM)
Colored toothpicks, seed beads, used coffee filters,
dowel rod, wooden block; piano hinge
PHOTO BY ARTIST

Alice Simpson

Rumba | 2002

11 ½ X 12 X 1 INCHES (29.2 X 30.5 X 2.5 CM)

Paste papers, Mylar, Japanese paper;
accordion binding; painted, calligraphy

PHOTO BY D. JAMES DEE

Erin Zamrzla

Untitled | 2006

6¼ X 4¾ X 1¼ INCHES (15.9 X 12.1 X 3.2 CM)

Handmade papers, book board, leather, beads, linen thread; sewn, hand beaded

PHOTOS BY ARTIST

Alice Austin

Milk, Butter, Eggs | 2004

8 X 6 X 5 INCHES (20.3 X 15.2 X 12.7 CM)

Rives lightweight, Mohawk cover-weight paper;
accordion binding; relief printed

PHOTOS BY ARTIST

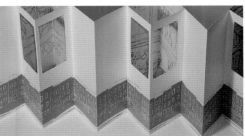

Bonnie A. Berkowitz

My Life as a Tree: Book Puppet | 2005

7 X 3 X 3 INCHES (17.8 X 7.6 X 7.6 CM)

Canson paper, cotton fabric, fleece, embroidery floss, glass beads, paper clay; origami-accordion fold; hand drawn, painted

PHOTOS BY CRAIG PHILLIPS

Erin Ciulla

Untitled | 2006

5¹/₂ X 7 INCHES (14 X 17.8 CM) EACH

Crocheted covers, wool, mohair yarn, handmade
paper, mixed fibers; long-stitch binding

PHOTO BY ROBIN TIEU

Judith I. Serebrin
House Hunting Scroll | 1994–95

8 X 17 X 1½ INCHES (20.3 X 43.2 X 3.8 CM)
Rives lightweight, wooden spindle, wood, watercolor, embroidery thread, bead; monoprints; sewn, painted, carved, etched
PHOTO BY ARTIST

Susan Kapuscinski Gaylord

Spirit Book #27: Absorbed Prayer | 2001

5 X 9¹/₂ X 9¹/₂ INCHES (12.7 X 24.1 X 24.1 CM)

Lotka paper, African Mashamba paper, thread,
glass seed beads, chestnut stems, binders board;
multiple signature books sewn on tapes; stitched

PHOTO BY DEAN POWELL

Cary Loving

Closed Chapter | 2006

8 X 4 X 10 INCHES (20.3 X 10.2 X 25.4 CM)

Clay, glaze, recycled book pages, cord

PHOTO BY TAYLOR DABNEY

Michelle Francis

Dos-a-Dos Times Two | 2004

4 1/8 X 3 3/8 X 3 INCHES (10.5 X 8.6 X 7.6 CM)

Flax, speckle tone, waxed linen thread;
Coptic, tacket, and long-stitch bindings

PHOTOS BY TOM MILLS

Nina Judin

Aimo | 2005

3 1/2 X 3 X 1 5/8 INCHES (8.8 X 7.5 X 4 CM)
Handmade paper, oak, feathers, parchment;
Romanesque binding; handwritten text

PHOTOS BY ARTIST

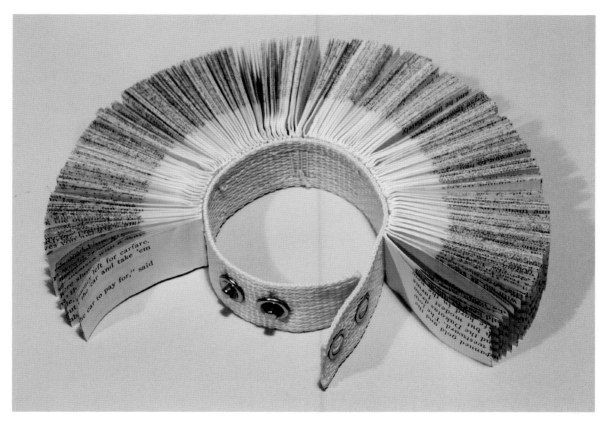

Michael A. Henninger

Book-let | 2000

5¹/₂ X 6¹/₂ X 1 INCHES (14 X 16.5 X 2.5 CM)

Paper, nylon strap, linen thread, metal snaps,
found book; repurposed signatures sewn on strap

PHOTO BY ARTIST

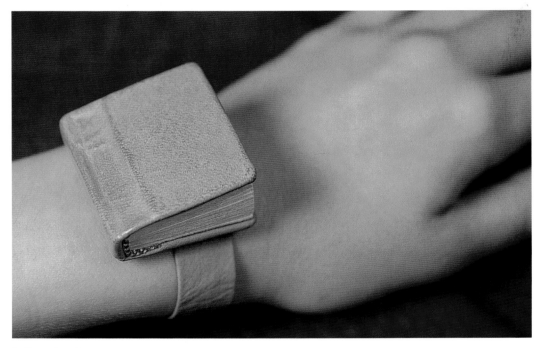

Julia Harrison

Wrist Book | 2000

1 1/2 X 1 1/4 X 1/2 INCHES (3.8 X 3.2 X 1.3 CM)

Leather, cotton paper, matte board, linen thread, Velcro,
Japanese endpapers, commercial headband, PVA; bound

PHOTO BY KEITH LOBUE

Mohamed Hassan Youssef Aly

Popular Signs, a Bookart | 2002

11 X 7⁷/₈ X 2³/₄ INCHES (27.9 X 20 X 7 CM)

Paste paper, recycled papers, handmade paper,
fabricated papers, leather

PHOTO BY ARTIST

Jean Buescher Bartlett

I Was On My Way Up The Stairs To See You | 2000–06

6 1/2 X 4 5/8 X 5/8 INCHES (16.5 X 11.8 X 1.6 CM)

Flax-paper covers, gouache; appliqué, embroidery,
letterpress, calligraphy by Nancy Leavitt

PHOTO BY JAY YOCIS

Susan Carol Messer

Terrain | 2004

8 X 6 X 1 INCHES (20.3 X 15.2 X 2.5 CM)

Moriki paper, book board, gold leaf;
accordion binding; inlaid, incised

PHOTOS BY ARTIST

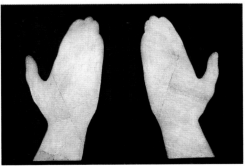

Lauren J. Campbell

Open Muse | 2005

5³⁄₄ X 4¹⁄₂ X ³⁄₄ INCHES (14.6 X 11.4 X 1.9 CM)

Faux leather, book board, handmade paper, vellum, linen thread; open spine, buttonhole, two slot

PHOTO BY ARTIST

Monique Lallier

The Pilgrim's Progress by John Bunyan | 1996

7¹⁄₂ X 5 X ³⁄₄ INCHES (19 X 12.7 X 1.9 CM)

Morocco leather, onlays; dos-a-dos binding;
embroidered, tooled, gilded

PHOTOS BY TIM BARKLEY

Lois Morrison

The Sisters Saw It Happen | 2005

11 1/8 X 13 1/2 X 3/4 INCHES (28.2 X 34.3 X 1.9 CM)

Fabric, metal, and other flat elephants; appliqué; transfer prints, woodcut and linoleum rubbings

PHOTOS BY CHARULATA DYAL

Jody Alexander

Max: Fused Shut VIII | 2002

4½ X 3 X 1¾ INCHES (11.4 X 7.6 X 4.4 CM)

Kozo paper, pen, ink; long-stitch binding; encaustic

PHOTO BY ARTIST

Steve Miller

Illegal Use of the Soul *by Luis Francisco Dìaz Sánchez,*
translated by Maria Vargas | 2006

5 1/8 X 4 X 3/8 INCHES (13 X 10.2 X 1 CM)

Recycled Cuban handmade paper, Biblio paper;
letterpress, photopolymer plates, linocuts

PHOTO BY ARTIST
LINOCUTS BY JULIO CESAR PEÑA PERALTA, HAVANA, CUBA
BOOKBINDING DESIGN BY ANNA EMBREE

Linda O'Brien
Opie O'Brien

Oaxacan Holiday | 2005

8¹/₂ X 9 X 4 INCHES (21.6 X 22.9 X 10.2 CM)

Board book, amate, handmade and specialty papers, silver coins, slide mount, watch vials, leather, milagros, matchbox, wire, beads, photos, stamps, found objects, copal incense; collage, transfer techniques, painting, airbrush, rubber stamps, embossing, wirework, knotting

PHOTO BY DINA ROSSI

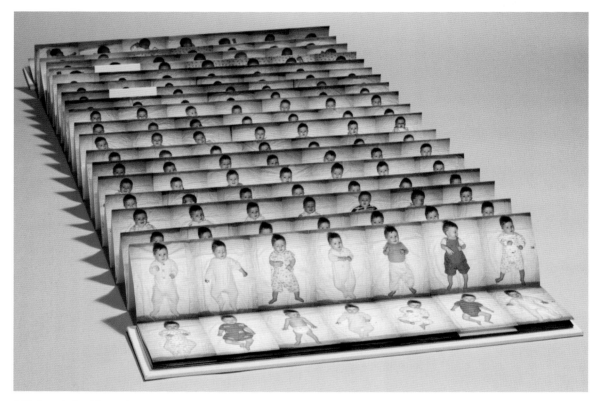

Michael A. Henninger

Oscar 365 | 2002

4 X 18³/₄ X 1¹/₄ INCHES (10.2 X 47.6 X 3.2 CM)
Paper; accordion binding; digital printing
PHOTO BY ARTIST

Crystal Cawley

Stone Women | 2006

10 X 8 X 3 INCHES (25.4 X 20.3 X 7.6 CM)

Old storybook pages, acrylic, various papers, mica dust, wood; Coptic binding

PHOTOS BY JAY YORK

Ana Garcés Kiley

Debajo de la Cama | 2004

3 X 30 X 1 INCHES (7.6 X 76.2 X 2.5 CM)

Arches paper, watercolor, ink; machine-screw binding

PHOTOS BY ARTIST

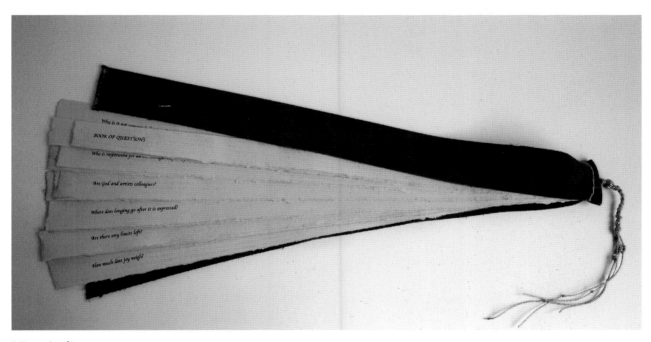

Nina Judin

Book of Questions | 2005

1¹/₄ X 16¹/₂ X ³/₈ INCHES (3.2 X 41.9 X 1 CM)

Paper, suede, feather, flax cord, silver beads;
Japanese binding; inkjet printed

PHOTO BY ARTIST

Susan Kapuscinski Gaylord

Spirit Book #30: Ixchel's Dream | 2002

5½ X 12 X 11½ INCHES (14 X 30.5 X 29.2 CM)

Mexican amatyl paper, banana mesquite paper, horn beads,
wood beads, thread, coconut shells, corn, binders board

PHOTO BY DEAN POWELL

Mohamed Hassan Youssef Aly

Old Leather Book | *2004*

11³/₄ X 8⁵/₈ X 2 INCHES (30 X 21.9 X 5 CM)

Paste paper, handmade paper, fabricated papers, leather
PHOTO BY ARTIST

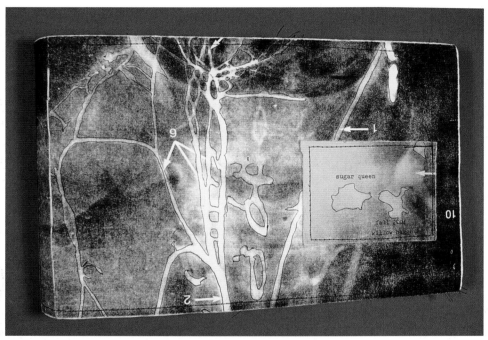

Willow Hagge

Sugar Queen | 2004

8 X 11 X 1 INCHES (20.3 X 27.9 X 2.5 CM)

Rives BFK, color photography;
hand and machine sewn; collaged
lithography, cyanotype

PHOTOS BY ARTIST

Amy Lapidow

Exposed Sewing Journals | 2006

6 X 7 X ¾ INCHES (15 X 17.5 X 2 CM)
Tyvek, handmade papers, acrylic;
joint construction, hand sewn
PHOTO BY DAVID CARRAS

Elizabeth Riggle

Rainbow Book | 2005

6 X 5 X 1½ INCHES (15.2 X 12.7 X 3.8 CM)

Ultra leather and hand-marbled paper, handmade paper; Coptic stitch, laguna binding

PHOTOS BY ARTIST

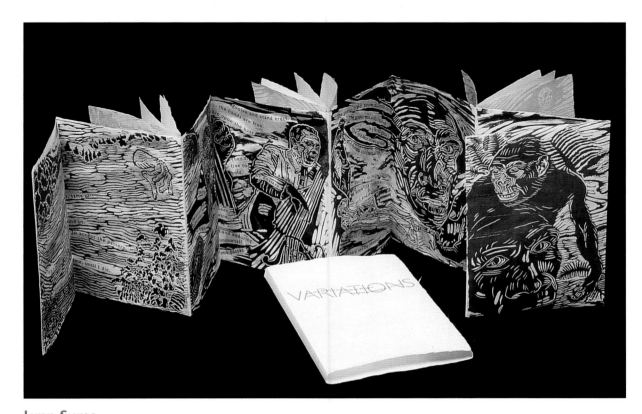

Lynn Sures

Variations on the Dialectic Between Mingus and Pithecanthropus Erectus | 2005

CLOSED: 10½ X 7½ X ½ INCHES (26.7 X 19 X 1.3 CM);
OPEN: 10½ X 60 INCHES (26.7 X 152.4 CM)

Abaca, hemp, linen thread, handmade paper; accordion binding and sewn-in pamphlet bindings; pulp painted, watermarked, letterpress, woodcut

PHOTO BY PRS ASSOCIATES

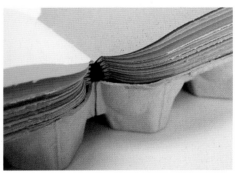

Erin Zamrzla

Half-Dozen | 2006

3½ X 6 X 4 INCHES (8.9 X 15.2 X 10.2 CM)

Egg carton, transparent and colored papers,
linen thread; Coptic binding

PHOTOS BY ARTIST

Kerri L. Cushman

Birdism Roulette | 2005

10 X 10 X 3 INCHES (25.4 X 25.4 X 7.6 CM)

Denim cast-paper eggs, abaca/wheat-straw crust;
transferred text fortunes

PHOTO BY JOHN WILLIAMS

Shanna Leino

Layover | 2005

1½ X 1¼ X 1 INCHES (3.8 X 3.2 X 2.5 CM)
Ebony, linen thread, hemp cloth;
Coptic binding; stitched, monoprint
PHOTO BY WALKER MONTGOMERY

Lynne Buschman

Arborae Borealis II | 2004

8 X 5½ X 8 INCHES (20.3 X 14 X 20.3 CM)

Found natural elements, encaustic wax, wood;
Coptic binding; collage

PHOTOS BY DENNIS CONNORS

Miriam Schaer

One Heart | 2004

14 X 17 X 9 INCHES (35.6 X 43.2 X 22.9 CM)

Indian handmade paper, silk, acrylic, girdle;
combination codex/accordion binding

PHOTO BY ARTIST

James Engelbart

Owls Are a Hoot | 2002

10½ X 8 X ¾ INCHES (26.7 X 20.3 X 1.9 CM)

Stonehenge Gray paper, Japanese bookcloth; Belgian secret binding; woodblock prints

PHOTOS BY ARTIST

Lindsey Mears

Fabre's Moth (Sixth Sense) | 2005

7 X 8¼ X 1¼ INCHES (17.8 X 21 X 3.2 CM)

Davey board, silk, metallic thread, acrylic; Victorian album binding; handset letterpress, bleached and toned cyanotypes

PHOTOS BY ARTIST

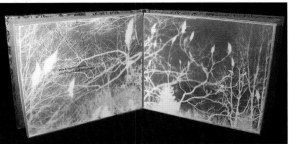

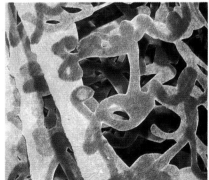

Robbin Ami Silverberg

Thoughts in the Form of a Letter | 2003

12¹/₄ X 9 X 1¹/₄ INCHES (31.1 X 22.9 X 3.2 CM)

Handmade paper, translucent abaca, Mylar pockets, silk
bookcloth; case binding, pulp painted, hand cut

PHOTOS BY GREGG STANGER

Melissa Sullivan

Untitled | 2004

5 X 3½ X 1½ INCHES (12.7 X 8.9 X 3.8 CM)

Ingres and overbeaten flax papers, calf leather, waxed
linen; herringbone stitch, cyanotype covers

PHOTO BY TOM MILLS

DOROTHY: IMAGES

Terry Horrigan

Dorothy: Images | 2001

8½ X 6¼ X ½ INCHES (21.6 X 15.9 X 1.3 CM)

Rives BFK; dos-a-dos binding,
accordion binding; letterpress

PHOTO BY ARTIST

Jerry Bleem

How to Enjoy the Final Mystery | 2005

4¹⁄₄ X 8¹⁄₄ INCHES (10.8 X 21 CM)

Cotton and kozo papers; stab binding;
letterpress, monoprints, embossed

PHOTOS BY ARTIST

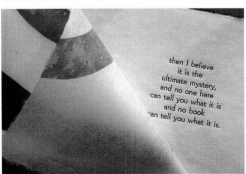

then I believe
it is the
ultimate mystery,
and no one here
can tell you what it is
and no book
can tell you what it is.

Chandler O'Leary

A Riddler's Compass | 2004

4 X 2½ X ¾ INCHES (10.2 X 6.4 X 1.9 CM)

Hahnemühle paper, Iris bookcloth, linen thread, watercolor; French folded, Coptic binding, nested box with hinged lids; letterpress, handset type, hand colored

PHOTO BY KARL LAUN

Jan Owen

Starfields | 2006

42 X 37 INCHES (106.7 X 94 CM)

Acrylic on paper, Tyvek; accordion binding;
hand lettered, painted, woven

PHOTOS COURTESY OF SEWANEE, THE UNIVERSITY OF THE SOUTH

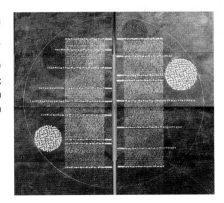

Inge Bruggeman

Bad News | 1998–99

11 X 7½ X ½ INCHES (27.9 X 19 X 1.3 CM)

Somerset paper; Coptic binding; letterpress,
hand-processed photopolymer plates, handset type

PHOTO BY BILL MORRISON

Marie Kelzer
Year 2000 Mass Media Mania | 1999

5½ X 6¼ X 1⅛ INCHES (14 X 15.9 X 2.8 CM)

Paste paper, black photo paper, dyed linen thread; limp binding, non-adhesive binding; sewn, laced, woven, laser printed

PHOTOS BY ARTIST

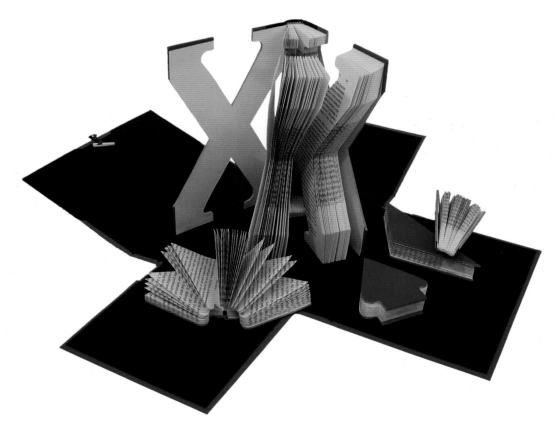

Jennifer Evans Kinsley

Exclusion | 2000

9 X 6 X 2 INCHES (22.9 X 15.2 X 5 CM)

Altered book, cloth, Canson cover stock, silk ribbon, bone closure, ink; perfect binding; saw-cut scroll

PHOTOS BY MICHELLE SALRIN STITZLEIN

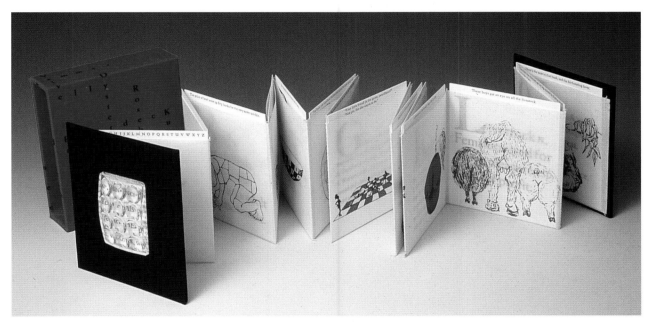

Diane Jacobs
Alphabet Tricks | 2000

4 X 3 1/2 X 3/4 INCHES (10.2 X 8.9 X 1.9 CM)

Kozo and Stonehenge papers, bookcloth, plastic
magnifier, silk thread; double-sided accordion
binding; stitched pockets, silkscreen, letterpress

PHOTOS BY ARTIST

Jackie Niemi

Blood Atlas | 1997

11 1/8 X 5 X 1 1/4 INCHES (28.2 X 12.7 X 3.2 CM)

Paper, museum board, color photocopies, linen thread; concertina binding; stitched, collage, cutouts

PHOTO BY ARTIST

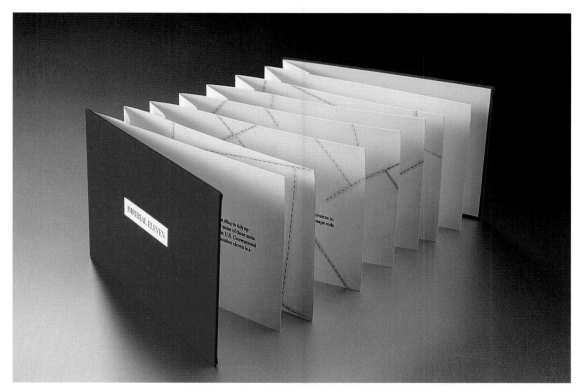

Stephanie Wolff

Imperial Eleven | 2004

4 1/8 X 6 3/16 X 3/4 INCHES (10.5 X 15.7 X 1.9 CM)

Papers, bookcloth, binders board; concertina binding with
attached pages; laser copy, watercolor, hand drawn

PHOTO BY JOHN SHERMAN

Cathryn Miller

Bipolar Dream Journal #2 | 2004

7 X 5 X 1½ INCHES (17.8 X 12.7 X 3.8 CM)

Cloth spine, handmade paper covers and endpapers, Fabriano Ingres textblocks, ribbon, linen thread; dos-a-dos binding

PHOTOS BY DAVID G. MILLER

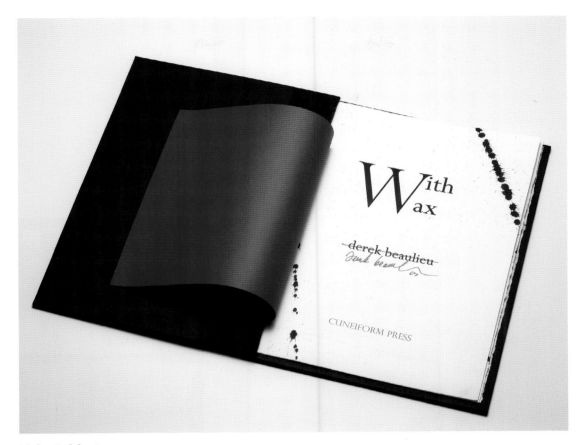

Kyle Schlesinger

With Wax by Derek Beaulieu | 2003

37¾ X 13½ X ⅜ INCHES (95.9 X 34.3 X 1 CM)

Suede, marker, acrylic ink, linen thread, binders board, binders cloth, Rives BFK, printers inks; Japanese binding; letterpress; hand splashed

PHOTO BY BIFF HENRICH

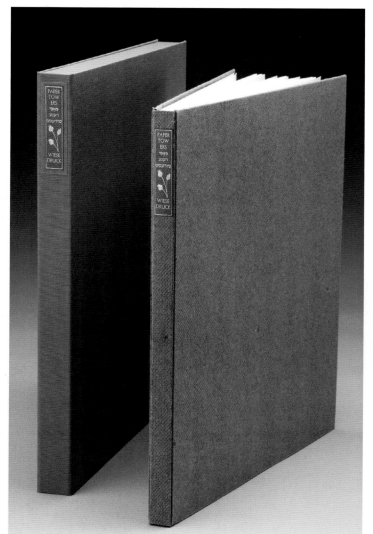

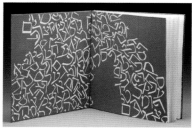

Sarah Horowitz

Paper Towers | 2005

12½ X 11¾ X 1 INCHES (31.8 X 29.8 X 2.5 CM)

Handmade Czech paper, Dutch windmill paper, leather, board, bookcloth, thread; hand bound; letterpress, lithography, woodcuts, engraving, linocut, stamping

PHOTOS BY BILL BACHHUBER

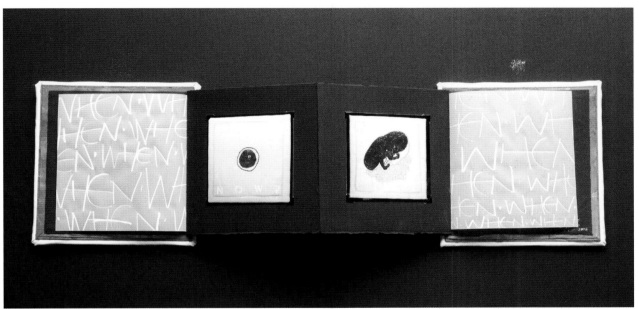

Rhonda Davies Ayliffe
When | 2006

9 X 8 5/8 X 1 3/16 INCHES (22.9 X 21.9 X 3 CM)

Arches, vellum, satin, glass beads, photo paper, gouache; accordion fold, dual pamphlet binding; hand beaded, machine quilted, calligraphy

PHOTOS BY BEN MARDEN

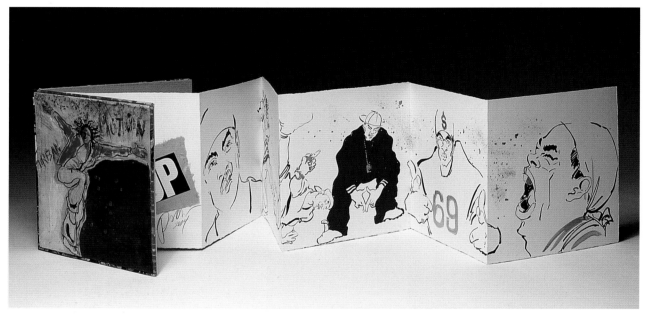

Alice Simpson

Urban Motion | 2004

OPEN: 12 X 10½ X 60 INCHES (30.5 X 26.7 X 152.4 CM)

Encaustic, wood covers, dowels, newspaper, India ink, gold, Arches paper; accordion binding; painted

PHOTOS BY D. JAMES DEE

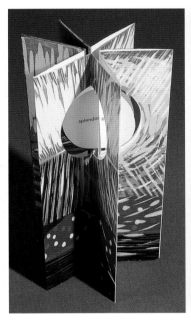

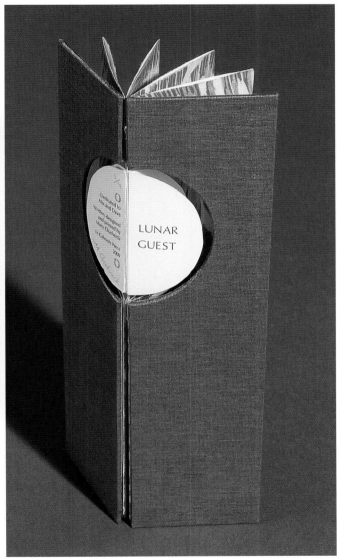

Macy Chadwick

Lunar Guest | 2000

9 1/2 X 2 1/2 X 1/4 INCHES (24.1 X 6.4 X 0.6 CM)

Mulberry paper, hard covers, cloth;
accordion book-in-book format;
color reduction woodcut, letterpress,
handset type

PHOTOS BY ANTHONY GEORGIS

Mary Ann Sampson

Then from All the Stones | 2004

9⅞ X 5¾ X ⅞ INCHES (25.1 X 14.6 X 2.2 CM)

Cheesecloth; Coptic binding, sewn signatures,
exposed guards; sgrafitto, letterpress,
collograph, handset type, painted

PHOTO BY ARTIST

Catherine Alice Michaelis

Volcano Blue | 1998

IN BOX: 17½ X 12 X 1 INCHES (44.5 X 30.5 X 2.5 CM)

Rives BFK, cotton thread; accordion binding, pamphlet stitched; linoleum prints, letterpress

PHOTO BY RICHARD NICOL

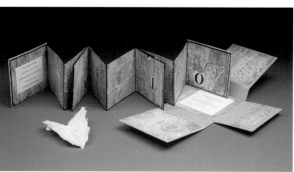

Liz Mitchell

Rough Waters/Blue Skies | 2005

CLOSED: 6 1/8 X 6 1/8 X 1/2 INCHES (15.5 X 15.5 X 1.3 CM)

Arches paper; accordion binding; linocut, collage

PHOTOS BY CRAIG PHILLIPS

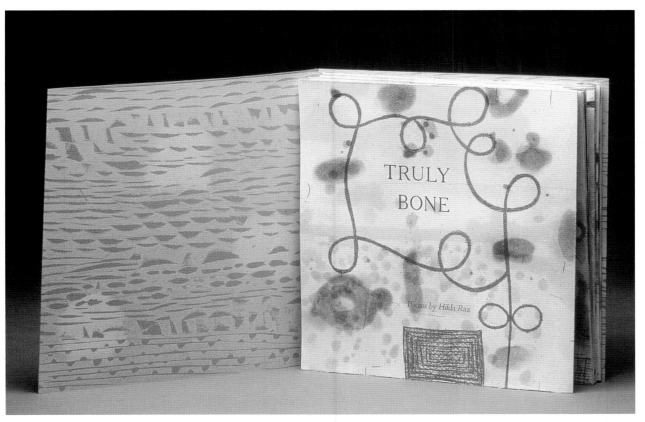

Karen Kunc

Truly Bone | 1999

CLOSED: 8 X 8 INCHES (20.3 X 20.3 CM)

Paper, ink; accordion binding;
letterpress, spitbite, etched

PHOTOS BY LARRY FERGUSON

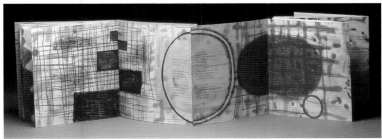

Alice Austin

Meatball Math | 2006

6 X 6 X 2 INCHES (15.2 X 15.2 X 5 CM)

Magnet, handset wood; handset wood
and metal type; map fold

PHOTO BY ARTIST

David John Lawrence

Tilt: A Skewed History of the Tower of Pisa | 2005

8¹/₄ X 6³/₁₆ X 1¹/₁₆ INCHES (21 X 15.7 X 2.7 CM)

Terra-cotta goatskin, paste paper by Catherine Levine, raised cords, semiprecious stones, sterling silver, 23-karat gold leaf, paste paper, acrylic paint; fine binding; colored, tooled, blackened, embroidered; stone setting by Steven Jay Coben

PHOTO BY BOBBY BADGER

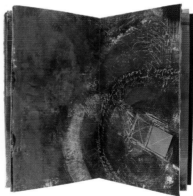

Dorothy Simpson Krause
Signs and Symbols | 2006

10 X 5½ X ½ INCHES (25.4 X 14 X 1.3 CM)
Paste paint, Reeves BFK, bookcloth;
sewn binding; printed, collage
PHOTOS BY ARTIST

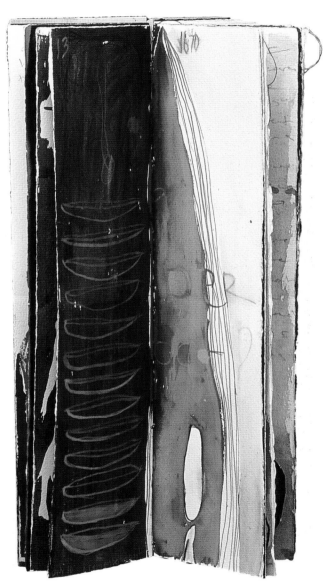

Jennifer Brook

*13 Generations: Do We
Remember a Boat?* | 2006

15 X 4 X 2 INCHES (38.1 X 10.2 X 5 CM)

Arches paper, found wood, ink, wax;
six-needle Coptic stitch

PHOTO BY STEVE MANN

Paula Jull

Hall of Dancers—Angkorwat | 2003

9 X 6½ X ¾ INCHES (22.9 X 16.5 X 1.9 CM)

Accordion binding, floating panels; inkjet printed

PHOTO BY ISU PHOTO SERVICES

Shu-Ju Wang

Nightmare Comes True | 2004

CLOSED: 5³/₄ X 6¹/₄ X ¹/₂ INCHES (14.6 X 15.9 X 1.3 CM)

Gouache, Rives BFK, Japanese paper

PHOTO BY ARTIST

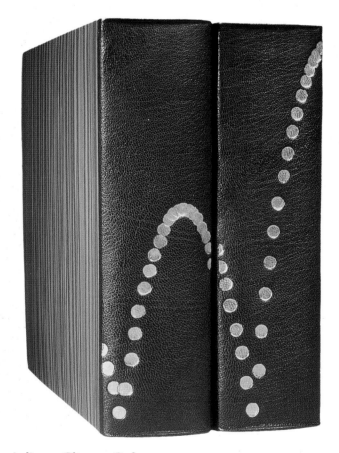

Juliayn Clancy Coleman

Motion Study | 2005

7½ X 10 X 2¼ INCHES (19 X 27 X 6 CM)

Paste paper, boards, goatskin, silk chevron
endbands, 23-karat gold; tooling

PHOTO BY SAVERIO TRUGLIA

Tara O'Brien

Tide Pools | 2005

4½ X 4¼ X 1½ INCHES (11.4 X 10.8 X 3.8 CM)

Elephant hide, Japanese paper, shells,
gold thread; Hedi Kyle's Panorama
structure; foil stamped

PHOTOS BY ARTIST

Beth Kennedy

Book of Epimetheus | 1991

CLOSED: 7¹/₂ X 7¹/₂ X 3¹/₂ INCHES (19 X 19 X 8.9 CM)

Telephone wire, plastic thread, rabbit fur, Mylar envelopes, fish, flowers, feathers, plywood, copper, sea urchin spine; sewn, woven, chiseled

PHOTOS BY ARTIST

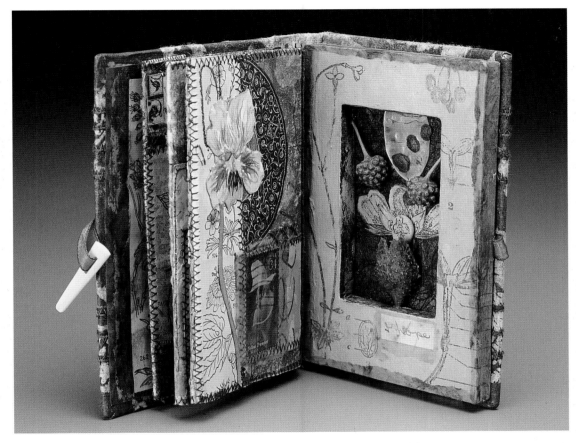

Sharon McCartney

See My Meaning | 2005

5³⁄₈ X 3³⁄₄ X 1 INCHES (13.7 X 9.5 X 2.5 CM)

Vintage book, rice paper, ephemera, decorative papers, watercolor, acrylic, thread, yarn, stamps, seeds and pods, bone clasp; interior accordion binding, attached signatures; stitched, painted, drawn, photocopy transfer, gelatin printing

PHOTO BY JOHN POLAK PHOTOGRAPHY

Beata Wehr

In Transit | 1998

9 X 9 X 1½ INCHES (22.9 X 22.9 X 3.8 CM)
Paper, acrylic paint, fabric, plastic,
wax, photographs, ink, linen, thread,
wheel; spiral binding
PHOTOS BY ARTIST

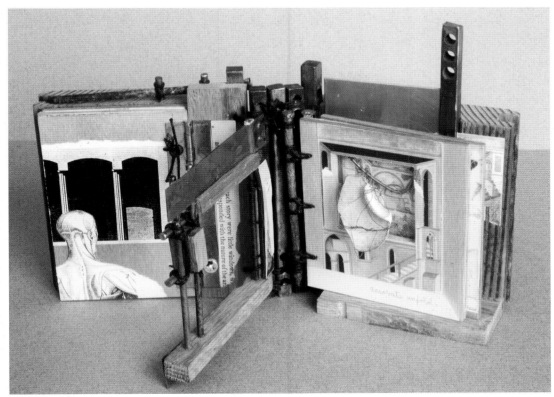

Susan Collard

Lyric Invention No. 1 | 2005

5 X 3½ X 3 INCHES (12.7 X 8.9 X 7.6 CM)

Board book, birch aircraft plywood, oak, reclaimed tongue-and-groove fir covers, metal, brass, waxed linen thread, paper, hardware; tied, mixed-media collage, handwritten text

PHOTOS BY ARTIST

Bonnie Thompson Norman

A Mealtime Blessing | 1995

11 1/4 X 8 1/2 X 1 1/2 INCHES (28.6 X 21.6 X 3.8 CM)

Wood covers, chipboard and kraft paper, paper
wrapper, fir box; hand-sewn binding; photoengraving,
letterpress, hand cut and sewn

PHOTO BY ARTIST

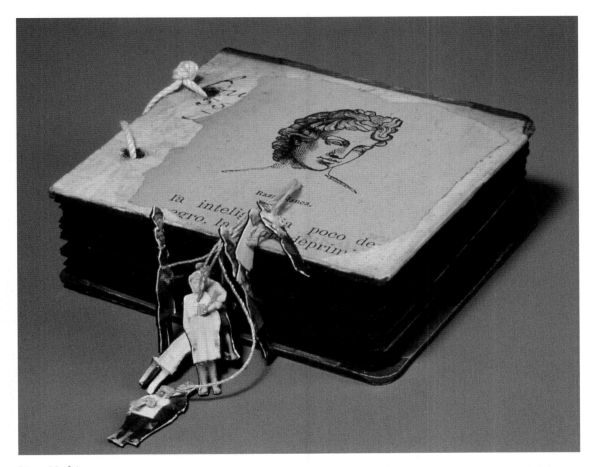

Lisa Kokin

Dormir, Dormirse, Morir | 2003

4½ X 3 X 1 INCHES (11.4 X 7.6 X 2.5 CM)

Found photos and text, paper, string; collage

PHOTO BY JOHN WILSON WHITE

Anna Embree

Byzantine Binding Model | 2005

9 X 6 X 2½ INCHES (22.9 X 15.2 X 6.4 CM)
Paper, wood, goat leather, cord, brass;
unsupported sewing; blind tooling
PHOTOS BY JILL TOBIN

Julie L. Johnson
Journey | 2006

6 X 4½ X 1½ INCHES (15.2 X 11.4 X 3.8 CM)

Handmade abaca and various papers, hickory bark,
waxed linen, copper pieces; stitched signatures

PHOTOS BY BRUCE McCAMMON

Krista Hanley
Post Card | 2004

CLOSED: 5³/₄ X 4¹/₈ X ³/₄ INCHES (14.6 X 10.5 X 1.9 CM)
Oiled paper, paper, board, photocopied antique postcards;
star-tunnel book format; hand painted, hand marbled
PHOTO BY STEVEN W. WALENTA

Jeanne Germani

Le Fleur | 2004

CLOSED: 6 X 5¼ X 2½ INCHES (15.2 X 13.3 X 6.4 CM)

Handmade papers, brown paper, found paper, matte board, leather, cotton thread, paste, found labels, decorative metal; sewn over tapes; painted, photo transfer

PHOTOS BY DAVID BRIGGS

Dorothy Field

Travels with Mary Ann/
Letter to the South | 2005

5³⁄₄ X 15 X 1 INCHES (14.6 X 38.1 X 2.5 CM)
Handmade natural-dyed kozo paper,
Arches paper, glassine, dry pigments;
accordion bound; photo transfer,
inkjet printed
PHOTO BY ARTIST

Cara N. Schlesinger

Sewn Cherry Prototype #1 | 2004

2¹⁄₂ X 2¹⁄₄ X 1¹⁄₂ INCHES (6.4 X 5.7 X 3.8 CM)
Cherry bark, Strathmore paper, brass strips, linen,
thread; stitched; hand-gathered and cured bark
PHOTO BY EUSTACIA MARSALES

Erin B. Gray

Cereology I | 2003

6 X 6 X 1½ INCHES (15.2 X 15.2 X 3.8 CM)

Sterling, fine silver, lead-bearing enamel, handmade paper, waxed linen, ink, paint, wood; Coptic binding; Cloisonné enamel, hand drawn, painted

PHOTO BY TIM BARNWELL

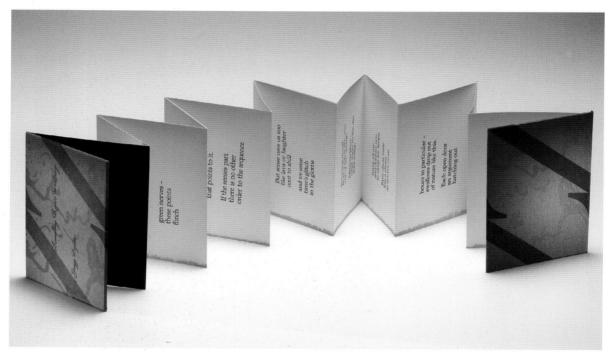

Kyle Schlesinger

Reading Keats to Sleep by Gregg Biglieri | 2003

4¹/₈ X 5¹/₈ X ³/₈ INCHES (10.5 X 13 X 1 CM)

Binders board, Fabriano paper, acrylic ink, colored pencils, multiple printer inks, archival glue; accordion binding; letterpress, painted, hand colored

PHOTO BY BILL HENRICH

Marian Crane

Plateau Guardians | 2004

3¹⁄₂ X 5³⁄₄ X 2¹⁄₂ INCHES (8.9 X 14.6 X 6.4 CM)

Leather, glass, beads, wooden box, tassels, red oak,
acrylic paint, linen, glass embroidery thread;
anchored, pierced, inlaid, beaded, embroidered

PHOTO BY ARTIST

Garrett Abe Izumi

Three Grey Women | 2003

6 X 6 X 1³/₄ INCHES (15.2 X 15.2 X 4.4 CM)

Rives heavyweight paper, Mexican bark paper,
oil-based relief ink; accordion binding; linoprint,
letterpress, lincocut, polymer plates

PHOTO BY ARTIST

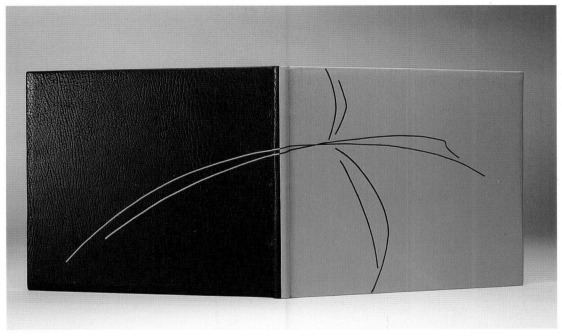

Monique Lallier

The Phoenix *by Alun Briggs, published by*
Old School Press, Bath, England, 1995 | 2003

9³/₄ X 8⁵/₈ X ¹¹/₁₆ INCHES (24.7 X 21.9 X 1.7 CM)
Goatskin, board, leather onlays,
paste endpapers, graphite, gold; sewn
PHOTOS BY TIM BARKLEY

Clarissa T. Sligh

What's Happening with Momma? | 1988

11 X 38¼ INCHES (27.9 X 97.2 CM)

Coventry and Stonehenge papers;
accordion binding; silkscreened, letterpress

PHOTOS BY D. JAMES DEE

Susan Hensel
My House | 1998

CLOSED: 8 X 5 X 2½ INCHES (20.3 X 12.7 X 6.4 CM)
Wasau and Canson papers, Fusion 4000 adhesive film,
Davey board, lignin-free cardstock, paint, putty; laser printed
PHOTOS BY KIM KAUFFMAN

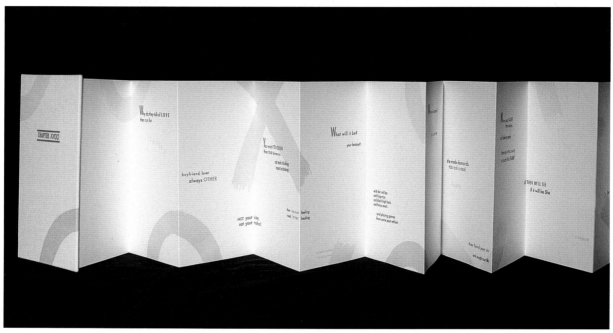

Mindy Belloff

Chapter XXOO | 2004

10 X 5 X ½ INCHES (25.4 X 12.7 X 1.3 CM)

Paper, bookcloth; letterpress, photopolymer
plates; written, designed, printed

PHOTOS BY ARTIST

Cynthia Lollis
Daniela Deeg
Nebbia | 2004

8 13/16 X 16 3/4 X 1 1/4 INCHES (22.5 X 42.5 X 3.2 CM)

Glama natural paper, wax thread, fabric,
grayboard box; stab binding; screen-printed

PHOTOS BY WALKER MONTGOMERY

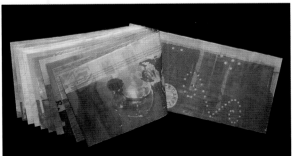

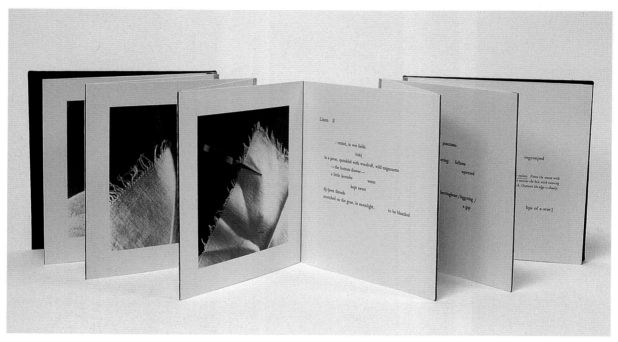

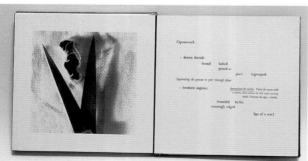

Paulette Myers-Rich

Broder | 1999

CLOSED: 6 X 6 INCHES (15.2 X 15.2 CM);
OPEN: 6 X 84 INCHES (15.2 X 213.4 CM)

Tiepolo, linen, boards; hand bound;
letterpress, inkjet printed

Gena M. Ollendieck

#3 Fork | 2004

10 X 12 X 5 INCHES (25.4 X 30.5 X 12.7 CM)

Stonehenge buff paper and handmade paper, calf leather, cotton cord, found objects; long-stitch multi-signature binding; inlaid, screw and elastic closure

PHOTO BY LARRY SANDERS

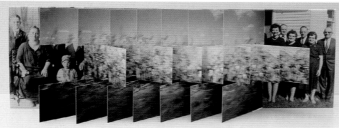

Karen Hanmer

Succession | 2002

CLOSED: 7 X 5 X ³/₄ INCHES (17.8 X 12.7 X 1.9 CM)
Pigment inkjet prints, flag book
PHOTOS BY ARTIST

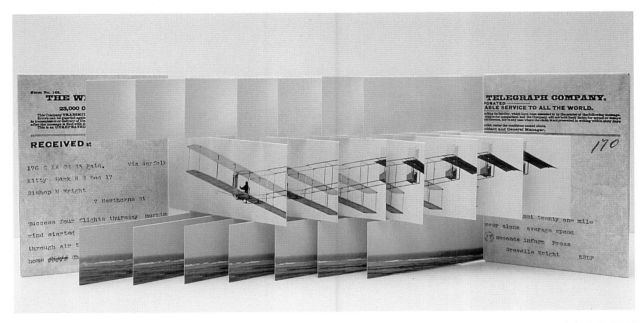

Karen Hanmer

They All Laughed | 2002

CLOSED: 7 X 5 X ¾ INCHES (17.8 X 12.7 X 1.9 CM)
Pigment inkjet prints, flag book

PHOTOS BY ARTIST

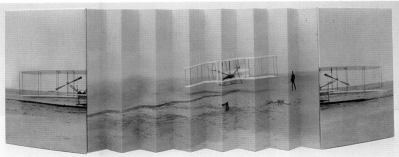

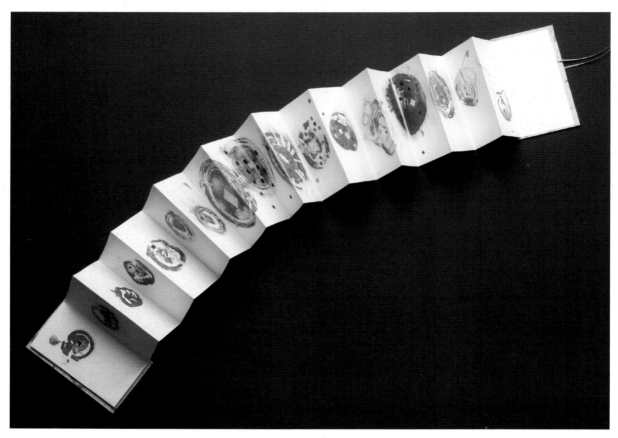

Rhonda Davies Ayliffe
Cells #2 | 2006

6¹/₄ X 69⁵/₈ INCHES (15.9 X 177 CM)

Mohawk, Unryushi papers, buttons, satin ribbon, ephemera;
accordion fold; acetone image transfer, collage

PHOTO BY BEN MARDEN

Robin Price

The Anatomy Lesson: Unveiling the Fasciculus Medicinae | 2004

14 X 10 X 1½ INCHES (35.6 X 25.4 X 3.8 CM)

Handmade cotton paper, elephant hide paper, over boards, hologram; concertina binding coproduced by Daniel E. Kelm; letterpress, photogravures, digital composition

PHOTO BY DEREK DUDEK

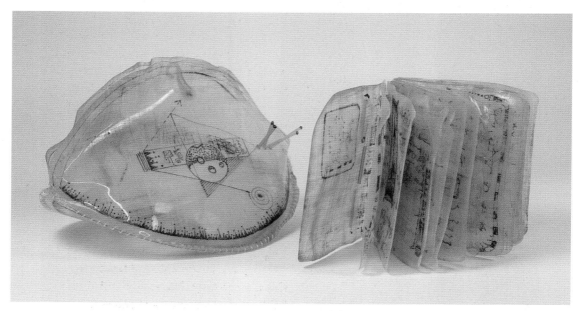

Peggy L. Johnston

Starship Log and Pod | 2004

LOG: 5 X 4 X 1 ½ INCHES (12.7 X 10.2 X 3.8 CM);
POD: 5 ½ X 9 ½ X 6 ¾ INCHES (14 X 24.1 X 17.2 CM)

Polyester, ink, crayon, fishing line, beads, eyelet;
Coptic binding; handwritten, drawn, heat warped

PHOTO BY LARRY JOHNSTON

About the Juror

Steve Miller
Illegal Use of the Soul *by Luis Francisco Dìaz Sánchez, translated by Maria Vargas* | 2006

Steve Miller
Design/Diseño *by Billy Collins, translated by Maria Vargas* | 2005

Steve Miller first studied the art of letterpress under the instruction of Walter Hamady. In 1976 he established Red Ozier Press, which has been recognized by several prestigious institutions for its fine craftsmanship of limited, first edition handmade books. Steve continues to publish limited edition works through Red Hydra Press. He teaches bookmaking, hand papermaking, and letterpress printing at the University of Alabama in Tuscaloosa. He also coordinates the university's MFA in the Book Arts Program. Steve has served in various leadership capacities related to hand papermaking and book arts. He recently traveled with a group of students and faculty to Cuba, where they collaborated with Cuban book artists on a volume of poems by former U.S. Poet Laureate Billy Collins.

Acknowledgments

It seems particularly appropriate to publish the work of book artists. Their contributions, quite gracefully displayed and photographed, make this book an homage to their individual and inspired labors.

Effusive thanks go to the two people whose efforts brought this book to fruition: Steve Miller—laid-back juror and handmade book artist by day, foodie and gadget guy by night—displayed great good humor throughout. Shannon Quinn-Tucker, dry wit at the ready and red pen in hand, helped the week fly by. Her steady and patient work, as the project's boundaries grew (and grew), deserves special and honorable mention; without her this book simply would not be.

Grateful appreciation also goes to fantastic designer Jackie Kerr, to master puppeteer Shannon Yokeley, Julie Hale, and to the rest of the stalwart Lark art crew. For this book especially, it took a village!

Suzanne J. E. Tourtillott

Contributing Artists

Adams, Alexis
Allston, Massachusetts
Pages 137 and 258

Adelman, Cathy
Malibu, California
Pages 181 and 204

Alexander, Jody
Santa Cruz, California
Pages 10, 66, and 335

Alotta, Sylvia Ramos
Berwyn, Illinois
Page 244

Aly, Mohamed Hassan Youssef
Abu Kir, Alexandria, Egypt
Pages 329 and 343

Antonacci, Sam Garriott
Seattle, Washington
Page 54

Austin, Alice
Philadelphia, Pennsylvania
Pages 3, 22, 175, 319, and 376

Ayliffe, Rhonda Davies
Cobargo, New South Wales, Australia
Pages 369 and 408

Bachelder, Debra Fink
Mount Gilead, Ohio
Page 280

Bailey, Alicia
Aurora, Colorado
Page 106

Barnes, Fairley
Santa Fe, New Mexico
Page 232

Bart, Harriet
Minneapolis, Minnesota
Page 51

Bartlett, Jean Buescher
Ann Arbor, Michigan
Page 330

Barton, Carol
Glen Echo, Maryland
Pages 35 and 198

Beech, Margaret
Haxby, York, United Kingdom
Page 224

Belloff, Mindy
New York, New York
Pages 52 and 402

Berkowitz, Bonnie A.
Bloomsbury, New Jersey
Pages 190 and 320

Berman, Harriete Estel
San Mateo, California
Page 157

Bird, Charlotte
San Diego, California
Page 82

Bivins, Chris
Enumclaw, Washington
Page 243

Blackmon, Nisa
Mahomet, Illinois
Page 240

Bleem, Jerry
Cicero, Illinois
Page 357

BonaDea, Artemis
Anchorage, Alaska
Page 147

Bond, Diane
Orchard Park, New York
Page 130

Bond, E.
Philadelphia, Pennsylvania
Pages 9 and 272

Borch, Ingrid Hein
Kelowna, British Columbia, Canada
Pages 21 and 208

Botnick, Ken
St. Louis, Missouri
Page 231

Brauhn, Molly Irene
Gainesville, Florida
Page 121

Braun, Katrin Kapp
Kirchheim-Teck, Germany
Pages 28 and 167

Broadfoot, Linda L.
Atlantic Beach, Florida
Page 250

Brook, Jennifer
Asheville, North Carolina
Page 379

Brown, Allison Cooke
Yarmouth, Maine
Page 23

Bruggeman, Inge
Portland, Oregon
Pages 115, 155, and 360

Buschman, Lynne
Montclair, New Jersey
Page 351

Bussolari, Barbara
Hayesville, North Carolina
Page 214

Calhoun, Cody
Springboro, Ohio
Page 286

Callahan, Nancy
Gilbertsville, New York
Page 75

Campbell, Carolee
Sherman Oaks, California
Page 170

Campbell, Joy M.
Santa Fe, New Mexico
Page 172